Glin Bayley

UNSTOPPABLE
WOMAN

———

Reveal the power of your heart
to create leadership impact and
cultivate confidence for the life you want

RETHINK PRESS

First published in Great Britain in 2020
by Rethink Press (www.rethinkpress.com)

© Copyright Glin Bayley

Heart on chapter openers by BomSymbols from Noun Project

Cover image © Nicola Fioravanti

This book is dedicated to my mum, the woman who inspired me to be unstoppable by being unstoppable.

And to my sister Rosie for always having my back, no matter what – a cheer squad that always keeps me going and helps me up every time I fall down.

I can't thank you both enough for all that you've done and continue to do for me – I love you.

Contents

Foreword

I met Glin in 2015 in my role of Chief Financial Officer (CFO) for George Weston Foods, one of Australia's largest food manufacturers. She had just transferred from London to Sydney to head up Finance for one of our sister companies, having built a great career and reputation over the course of 14 years in various finance roles.

I met a smart, determined and driven lady who had her sights firmly set on achieving her goal of becoming a Finance Director/CFO.

Over the next few years we met regularly to discuss business strategy and to share personal insights. Our conversations would often include Glin's career and personal development. She embraced the opportunity to discuss issues with someone external to her business and with exposure to other parts of the company as well as previous experience in CFO roles at McDonalds, KFC and in Media. It was wonderful to share insights and strategies that have helped me during my career.

I feel honoured to have contributed by planting some of the seeds that germinated and grew into the valuable insights and personal stories that are shared in *Unstoppable Woman*. I have a strong sense of obligation to 'pay it forward' by coaching and advocating for women climbing the career ladder.

One thing I've learnt is we have to find a way to bring our authentic selves to the table and fundamentally be true to who we are if we are going to get real satisfaction from what we do and achieve. I also believe that to do this we need to spend more time understanding ourselves and what makes us tick. Whether it is for personal discovery, a career shift or to improve your self-leadership (and leadership in general), *Unstoppable Woman* will provide the map to navigate this path.

Glin's has drawn on her experiences growing up with a single mum, working as a finance executive and more recently running her own executive coaching business to create the H.E.A.R.T. self-leadership method. The concepts themselves are not new, but Glin has built them into a logical framework that is easy to understand and follow. Her personal and **open** vulnerable anecdotes and real-life experiences bring the concepts to life in meaningful and helpful ways.

FOREWORD

During my own thirty-year career, I have worked with many people. Some have been incredible sponsors, coaches and cheerleaders who have provided me with career and personal development opportunities I did not think I was capable of. For these I am grateful. That said, there have been difficult, stressful periods too. One being when I was forced to go on my own journey of self-discovery to examine myself, the value I bring to the table and building the courage to use my voice. Glin will inspire and help you to find and use yours too - it is so much more fulfilling to leverage our talents, use our voices and find that seat at the table.

As I write this in 2020, I am sobered by how the world has been turned on its head by a global pandemic. I appreciate that taking a radical career or personal move might not be an option right now. What is available, though, is to take this time of great change and use it for deeper self-reflection using Glin's self-leadership method.

While this new normal presents us with our own set of challenges (anxiety, social isolation and uncertainty) we can make this a defining event that makes us stronger and better people.

So many women are like the characters in the *Wizard of Oz*, looking for external magic to give us qualities we already have, but do not yet see.

I really hope that as you work through *Unstoppable Woman* you discover your own magic and use this as an opportunity to build awareness of who you are and what you want, and to find that seat at the table.

Lorna Raine
CFO, George Weston Foods

Introduction

*The old woman I shall become will be
quite different to the woman I am now.
Another I is beginning.*
George Sand

Who are you?

This book is not about changing who you are: this book is about *discovering* who you are. The biggest enemy you face is not outside of you but one that resides deep within, one that holds you hostage and limits your potential to be the Unstoppable Woman you were born to be.

I've written this book for you as well as for me. It captures the lessons that have been hard-won, through the loss of loved ones, the ending of relationships and the shattering of dreams. Each experience has revealed more and more of who I am at my core. I realise now that if it weren't for this journey, you wouldn't be reading this book, and I would not have learned what it truly means to be unstoppable.

If you've picked up this book, this is who I believe you are. You're an established, ambitious female leader with high aspirations, not just for your career but more broadly. You feel you have a deeper purpose to fulfil, but things keep getting in the way of you realising your dreams, and you find it frustrating. You know there is more for you out there, but don't know how to access it.

Three main things that might be holding you back are a lack of time, a lack of energy and, most critically, a lack of inner confidence – even if you do appear to present a confident exterior. You desire to make a real impact for good with your life.

Is this your world? You generally lack time because you are overstretched both at work and home and rarely get a moment to yourself; you always put others' needs first. You lack energy because you struggle to say no and find it hard to set and keep boundaries both professionally and personally to stay ahead and be appreciated. Limited time for self-care means your cup is often emptied as you fill others' cups.

While you present yourself confidently on the outside, your inner critic is all too audible. She constantly makes you doubt yourself: every time you think you have silenced her, she shows up again. Unfortunately, your perfectionism and self-doubt often leave you paralysed and missing out on the life you really want. I imagine that you've worked hard and are successful by most societal measures, yet you probably experience some level of imposter syndrome. You don't want to get things wrong and be found out not to be good enough.

As an ambitious and results-driven leader, do you find yourself easily getting stuck on a merry-go-round without checking that it's the one you want to be on? Do you feel that you want more for yourself beyond just work? Would you know how to achieve it without compromising your professional life? Or does it feel too late to change anything anyway?

This book will teach you a lot about yourself and you will learn how to get what you want by connecting with who you are. If you are looking to improve your life, then you'll get immense value from the principles I share.

It's worth saying, however, that if you expect the usual leadership and impersonal business book, this won't be for you. While leadership is at the heart of this book, I share many real-life stories which are applicable in business. The path I've taken with this book is to look at life leadership – *your* life leadership.

This book will take you on a journey of self-discovery to reconnect you to who you are on the inside. It will help you reveal the power of your heart to create the impact you want. You will become unstoppable as you unlock more time, energy and confidence for the life you want.

Who am I?

I'm someone like you. I'm someone who had to lose themself before I could find myself.

I had an impressive career working in finance for several global blue chip companies. But in the seventeen years I spent striving for a Chief Finance Officer (CFO) role, not once did anyone ask me if I believed it would make me happy. As a qualified management accountant, I'd spent my twenties and early thirties focused on climbing the corporate career ladder, but deep down I knew I wasn't truly fulfilled. I came from a low socio-economic background and single-parent household. My greatest advantage was my mum. She made huge sacrifices so that I could have a better start in life than her and learn how to stand on my own two feet.

As a result of my upbringing, I felt that I had something to prove. I wanted to build a secure life for myself given the sacrifices my mum made. That's what I did by following a career in finance. It was only when my marriage ended that I found myself lost and questioning the purpose and meaning of life. When I reflected on how I managed to emerge from this heartbreak and observed the life changes I made, I realised that these achievements came about through understanding my heart and following where it was leading.

I moved to the other side of the world in my mid-thirties and started over. I found the courage to be honest with myself and leave my corporate career in finance to start my own business doing what fulfils me, rather than what I thought I should be doing. I realised that I was just working to prove that I was worthy enough and smart enough to be a CFO.

I often joke that my namesake is Glinda, the Good Witch in the *Wizard of Oz* (although my full name, Glinder, is spelled slightly differently). I always remember her wise words to Dorothy, 'You always had the power, my dear, you just had to learn it for yourself.'

That's the lesson I believe we all have to learn.

As a result of taking my own journey of self-discovery and transforming my life, I now coach female corporate executives using the self-leadership method I share in this book. I also connect female leaders through my female leadership workshops which focus on helping them to reveal the power of their hearts and be unstoppable in creating the life and leadership they want.

I spent too long living the life I thought I should be living instead of the life that, at heart, I knew I wanted. This has inspired me to help others avoid wasting time doing the same.

Since moving out of finance into executive coaching, I've learned a lot about female leaders. It's scary observing how time and time again they face the same challenges. Often, they are aware of their lack of time, energy and confidence, but what I usually find is that these are just superficial challenges. The real challenge is the disconnection from themselves – who they really are and what they really want.

The women I've worked with usually come to me for help in navigating their leadership roles and careers, but often the career isn't the root issue. It's nearly always what's happening in their personal lives and the quality of the relationship they have with themselves that they need to focus on.

As a consequence, my work can vary: from helping one client prepare her mindset to having a baby after several failed IVF attempts to assisting another with leaving her corporate role to start a new business in a completely different field; from preparing a client land a promotion for an executive role she didn't believe she could do to demonstrating to another that she could lead a team in a country where she didn't speak the language.

I'm a great believer that if we each reveal the power of our hearts, female leaders would have an equal place at any table and could create a new paradigm for the way women work and lead. That's what I hope to inspire through this book.

My promise to you

I share a raw and vulnerable account of my journey of self-discovery. By using the method I created for self-leadership, I show how it transformed my life. I believe that a guide can only take you to where they've been themselves, so be prepared for an honest and truthful account of the good, the bad and the ugly in my own journey to becoming an 'Unstoppable Woman'.

I sometimes feel slightly indulgent talking about myself – no holds barred. I've never been one for self-promotion, but something I've learned over recent years, perhaps a by-product of turning forty, or maybe just another life truth that took a little longer to sink in, is that if I don't see how phenomenal I am, then how the hell can I convince you to see how phenomenal you are?

I hope that sharing my own journey inspires you to discover the truth of the Good Witch Glinda's words, that it's something you have to learn for yourself.

I know how much I love to listen to other people's stories and learn from them. My friends would describe me as someone who is easy 'to do a deep and meaningful with'. I hope I can help you find your voice by sharing my own story.

You have within you the power of your heart to be unstoppable. You've probably covered up this power and forgotten how to access your inner wisdom.

My intention is to help you align your heart and mind so that you can discover your own truth, reconnect with yourself and begin to see how unstoppable you are.

Every journey begins with a first step

Before we dive into the heart of this book, I thought it might be helpful to share a little about where my journey began. There will be many more insights into my life and the lessons I've learned, including how my upbringing shaped me, how I navigated the end of my marriage and my move to the other side of the world. It also describes how I left corporate life to make the leap to start my own business, my experience of mental illness and my journey to self-trust. I describe how I navigated these life challenges and how they taught me more about myself than I could ever imagine.

Let's begin with the first step on this path – the discovery of who I am.

Feeling lost was not something I'd ever experienced, but when my marriage ended that was exactly how I felt. From a young age my dreams had centred around getting married and having babies, so when I found myself facing single life six months short of my thirty-fifth birthday, I couldn't quite comprehend my new situation.

I had celebrated the start of 2014 with the news that we were expecting our first baby. After several years of trying naturally, we accepted the eye-watering costs and went down the IVF route. I can't begin to describe the elation we felt at finally hearing the news that we had desperately hoped for. Unfortunately, our high didn't last long as I miscarried before the twelve-week scan. The grief we experienced was overwhelming and the numbness that followed felt like it would last forever. Slowly, with the help of counselling, the fog that surrounded us began to lift. But along with that clarity came new questions about our future. While I was beginning to feel excited and energised for our next chapter, my husband was wrestling his inner demons and battling with his own personal needs.

Shortly afterwards we took the tough decision to part ways. This was terribly sad and even harder to navigate because we still had so much love for each other. My sense of loss was all-consuming, trying to comprehend that I'd started the year with a husband and a baby on the way, and was now facing the end of the year single. Wow.

I felt the loss not only of the relationship we had, but also of the dreams I had for our future. I had imagined growing old together, sitting on a bench overlooking the sea somewhere in the south of England, holding hands and sharing a bag of chips! The separation also meant acknowledging and saying goodbye to my hopes of being a mother, at least for the foreseeable future. It was a triple blow.

I hadn't realised how much my sense of personal identity had been wrapped up in being a wife and a partner. Now that I was on my own, I faced a huge question – who was I?

I didn't know the answer. I was no longer a wife or a partner, nor was I the same single person I had been before I met my husband. So much had changed, and I felt I was back in life's starting blocks. Only this time I didn't feel as excited about exploring the new adventures that lay ahead of me, as I had in my twenties. I felt scared and apprehensive about what was to come. All the certainty in my life had been replaced by uncertainty; this feeling of being out of control was new to me.

As I was struggling to make sense of it all I reached out to my family and close friends and shared how I was feeling. I've always found it easy to share what's on my mind with the people closest to me, but I wasn't consciously aware at the time that it was because I am comfortable with vulnerability. They helped me see things a little more clearly at a time when I didn't know which foot to put in front of the other. While they couldn't tell me who I was, they could share with me what I meant to them and how they saw me. They also reminded me of all the other dreams I'd talked about over the years, the ones I'd forgotten and put aside when we started trying for a family.

My mum reminded me of a dream I'd had in my early twenties, which I had let go of, thinking it would never happen – to live and work in Australia. As I sit and write this book, it's January 2020 and I want to pinch myself because I'm now a permanent resident of Australia and have been living in Sydney for nearly five years. My dream did come true. I'll share more about how it happened later.

Achieving this dream didn't answer the question of who I am, but it did show me what I am capable of when I focus on something. For the last five years that's exactly what I've been doing – focusing my attention on discovering who I really am and creating the life I want.

I've observed what makes me happy and what doesn't. I've listened carefully to my intuition to tell me what is right for me and what isn't. I've spent a lot of time learning how to love myself the way I love others and feeling nourished by the kindness I extend to myself. I've taken up new hobbies and dropped some along the way, paying close attention to the signals my body sends ahead of my brain when something doesn't connect to my soul. Most importantly, I've learned to be honest with myself and consciously embrace everything I previously considered to be my weaknesses. Instead, I consider how these weaknesses could in fact be strengths and superpowers.

Although I've always been naturally comfortable with vulnerability, I'd always considered it my Achilles heel. I wear my heart on my sleeve and sometimes that means I get hurt. Whether in my personal life or in business, vulnerability is often regarded as something negative, a sign of weakness that could be exploited. Every time I tried to present myself differently, perhaps as a much tougher and more stoic individual, it felt yucky and insincere. I gradually realised that it was more painful for me to hold myself back than face the risk of someone hurting me because of my vulnerability. Brené Brown, a researcher and storyteller, defines vulnerability as uncertainty, risk and emotional exposure.[1] Writing this book and sharing my personal story are the most vulnerable things I've ever done. I'm *uncertain* about how it will be received by you, the *risk* of judgement is certainly high and *emotional exposure* is pretty much guaranteed. Bearing in mind the definition of vulnerability, and Brené's words ringing loud and clear, I would like to explore the idea of courage. I see courage in facing this uncertainty, courage in taking a risk and courage in acknowledging that while emotional exposure is likely, I feel it is necessary. I recognise that by being vulnerable myself I am showing you it's OK to be vulnerable too. Why? Because you can't access who you are on the inside without being vulnerable, and life is too short to be anyone other than your true self.

For me, courage = vulnerability. If you ever find yourself thinking that being vulnerable is a weakness, stop and remember what courage it takes to let yourself be vulnerable.

---

1   https://brenebrown.com

The last five years of focusing on myself and seeking the answer to the question 'Who am I?' have led me to the most powerful answer.

Quite simply, I discovered, I am.

ONE

The Power Of Heart

Dare to connect with your heart. You will be lifting not only yourself and those you love and care about, but also the world in which you live.
Doc Childre, HeartMath Founder

The power of heart is phenomenal and the science I delve into in this chapter will demonstrate how much our hearts can influence our lives and help us to create the lives we want.

First, however, I want to share the story about when I first learned about the power of heart – through my mum.

An Unstoppable Woman

What if you came home after finishing work one day to find that your house had been burgled? Only at second glance do you see that it isn't quite what you thought – you notice some of the stolen items have been replaced.

One afternoon over three decades ago that's exactly what happened to my mum.

My parents' families came from India, where arranged marriages are common practice. My dad grew up in England, but my mum was raised in India, and only left at the age of twenty-three when her marriage had been arranged. The first time she met my dad was when she arrived at London's Heathrow Airport. Luckily for her she thought he was good-looking.

Fast forward four years and she was married with two young daughters – me, aged three, and my sister, aged one.

After finishing work and picking us up from the baby-sitter, my mum returned to a house that at first glance looked like it had been burgled. But something wasn't quite right. My parents didn't have much money; Mum worked full time and was slowly furnishing the house with her income, buying new appliances when she could afford them. But as she walked into the lounge from the hallway, she noticed that the new TV and video player had gone. As she moved to the kitchen she was even more baffled. In place of the new refrigerator stood a refrigerator half the size and considerably older. At that moment it dawned on Mum that they hadn't been burgled at all and the only other person with keys to the house was my dad.

As she looked around the kitchen, Mum remembered the money hidden under her mattress. She ran upstairs and, as she suspected, it was gone. So too had the new bed she had bought; in its place, as you might have guessed, was an old one.

My mum soon discovered that my dad had decided that he'd had enough of playing grown-ups. He had moved back in with his parents, taking the things he wanted with him and leaving behind everything he didn't – including us.

That day our lives changed forever. My mum found herself presented with a choice: *to lose herself* by dwelling on what she had just lost, which was significant – her husband, her savings, her identity as a wife, her hopes and dreams of a future with the man she loved – or *to find herself by* recognising her value and acknowledging that her purpose was much greater than her fears.

The day my dad chose to leave, my mum chose to stay.

She became focused, organising for the locks to be changed the same day, so that my dad couldn't take the gas cooker, the only remaining valuable item which she really needed.

She had an incredibly tough job bringing up two daughters on her own in a foreign country. My mum didn't speak English (she grew up on a farm in rural India), yet she ensured that my sister and I got the best education we could. She saved and bought her own home and slowly replaced all the things that my dad had taken. She showed us how to stay strong in the face of adversity and to see the possible in the impossible.

She created an environment at home that was full of love and joy and to this day continues to support me and my sister in any way she can.

I have no doubt there were days, in the early years, when she felt she couldn't go on. Her parents were in India and she didn't have a support network around her. She was raising two daughters on her own with no financial or emotional support from my dad. Mum turned to her faith to see her through the darkest days, and she continues to show appreciation every day for surviving the times when she didn't have enough money to put food on the table.

I cannot express enough how grateful I am for my mum choosing her purpose over her fears. Her purpose, in case it isn't clear, was raising my sister and me. She could have quite easily lost herself; it would have been totally understandable given the circumstances. But her resilience, determination and resourcefulness have showed me time and time again that a clear purpose is significantly stronger than any fear.

What I learned through my mum's journey was that she fulfilled her purpose by unlocking the power of her heart. Her head alone would not have got her through the loneliness, the social isolation, the language barrier and the loss of connection to the community she was raised in.

The power of her heart tapped into a deep well of energy that allowed her to take action and cultivate the resilience required to succeed despite the odds she faced. She had unshakeable trust in her faith and also in herself. For me, she epitomises an Unstoppable Woman.

I have heartfelt appreciation for the gift that she gave me, the gift of her love every single day, a gift she continues to give.

If you asked yourself today, 'What if my purpose is stronger than my fear?', what would the power of your heart enable you to do that you've been afraid of so far? What would you strive for, knowing that purpose always trumps fear?

I'm glad my mum showed me the power of her heart and chose to create a new life for us. Life doesn't always unfold in the way we expect or hope, but we have a choice. To quote a line from my favourite film, *The*

Shawshank Redemption, we can either 'get busy living or get busy dying' – your choice.

Power-of-Heart science

OK, time for the science. I included this section because I want to demonstrate, for those who need a little more convincing, that the concepts I share in this book are grounded in research and science.

While my own approach to life is through harnessing my intuition, something I've improved at significantly over the last few years, I do recognise from my many years in finance that data and facts to support a perspective are necessary to connect the dots.

There are two things I want you to acknowledge about your heart. First, it is a vital organ for living – ultimately there is no getting away from the fact that when your heart stops, you stop. You need to take care of it. I know I'm stating the obvious, but it's necessary to remind our-selves of the obvious because it's easy to take things for granted.

Second, your heart is a powerful source of inner know-ing and guidance. You might call this intuition – it is ultimately your inner power.

I know this might sound a little 'woo-woo', so here's the science for the geek in you. This is your chance to find out just how powerful your heart is in revealing your own insight about the life you want.

Let's start with the definition of intuition. 'Intuition is the ability to understand or know something without the need for conscious reasoning.'[2]

We can sometimes experience intuition like an 'aha' moment where things begin to make sense in a way we didn't see before. We had the implicit knowledge but now the dots have connected. Or we experience intuition as a feeling, call it a hunch, like a mother who intuits what her baby needs although it can't yet speak. It can be knowing when two people have had an argument just from sensing the energy in the room. Sometimes we experience intuition in a way that we can't make sense of rationally. An example of this would be a 'sense of knowing' that someone you love who lives on the other side of world needs help. You phone them and discover that they have been unwell in hospital. You don't know how you 'knew' something was wrong, but you had an intuitive nudge to make the call.

Intuition can be incredibly powerful, and it can be accessed more readily when you know how.

Most of us have an inner belief, a kind of knowing, that our hearts yield great power. Often in our outer world, and in the corporate environments we work in, we assert

2   www.lexico.com/en/definition/intuition

that our brains rank higher than our hearts. If we allow ourselves to see the heart's true power, we might revise this view.

The HeartMath Institute was founded in 1991 and has been studying the connection between heart and brain for nearly thirty years, with considerable scientific research on understanding the power of the heart.

They found that the heart's rhythm pattern is the best reflection of our inner state and their research demonstrates that through greater heart coherence (when heart, mind and emotions are in sync) we can access the heart's intuition, improve our mental and emotional wellbeing, and make better life decisions and day-to-day choices.

In one study by the HeartMath Institute, they measured participants' heart rhythm and reactions to a set of random images designed to arouse an emotional reaction of either distress or calm. They discovered that the heart received intuitive information about the images about to be shown and that the participants' heart rhythm responded to the images a full six seconds *before* they appeared on the screen. In the same study they also found evidence that women were more attuned to intuition of the heart than men.[3]

---

3   www.heartmath.org/research/research-library/intuition/
electrophysiological-evidence-of-intuition-part-1

The heart has access to information outside the boundaries of time and space. It's been proven beyond a shadow of a doubt.[4]

Rollin McCraty PhD, one of the original founders of HeartMath

This scientific research shows us that our hearts intuitively know what is good for us and is helpful for those who need further convincing. We often find it difficult to explain the sense of knowing because it is intelligence beyond the physical world we know, but it doesn't make it any less valid.

Given that we often struggle to accept things that appear 'irrational', the work of the HeartMath Institute is focused on addressing heart/mind incoherence. This is the split between the heart and mind that many of us might recognise and feel when they are not aligned.

HeartMath studies have shown that by taking charge of how you feel and thereby changing the pattern of your heart rhythm through greater heart coherence, you can access significant benefits. These include:

- 24% improvement in the ability to focus

- 30% improvement in sleep

- 38% improvement in calmness

---

4 www.gaia.com/article/mysteries-of-the-human-heart

- 46% drop in anxiety

- 48% drop in fatigue

- 56% drop in depression[5]

Imagine the value that you could create – as an Unstoppable Woman – leading a business environment that harnessed the power of the heart, one that acknowledged heart coherence (alignment of heart, mind and emotions) as a key facilitator of wellbeing, and thereby long-term sustainable performance.

If we acknowledge the magnificent intelligence of our hearts and allow ourselves to tune into our own heart's power, the results could be phenomenal.

My heart intuition

I've become a big believer in trusting the timing of my life. As frustrating as it can be, I've learned to recognise that in life it's easier to go with the flow than trying to swim upstream.

An example of this is when I started to write this book almost three years ago. Each time I sat down to write, after about several thousand words I would get stuck. I didn't really know what I wanted to get across in the

---

5   www.heartmath.com

book, although I knew I wanted to write it. I struggled to structure it in a way that would be of value and not read like it was just ramblings in my journal.

So, I stopped. I trusted that I would eventually write my book; I didn't concern myself too much about the timing. As I look back, I'm so I'm glad I didn't write it then or battle to finish what I'd started several times. It would have been a completely different book. I now see clearly that there was much more for me to experience in my journey of self-discovery before I would be able to help others.

My book is based on my self-leadership method, but the method didn't come to me in a conventional way. Like the intuition I described earlier, it came to me in a flash of insight, an 'aha' moment when the dots connected.

I was preparing a short TED-style presentation as part of a professional speaker year-long training programme. It was coming up to the final bootcamp and my presentation was to be in front of a number of agents from speakers' bureaus. I was feeling the pressure. Over the duration of the year, the initial topics I'd been speaking on had changed and I didn't feel as connected to them.

I'd been procrastinating and with one week to go; I still had no clue what I wanted to speak about. Not only did I have to determine my topic, I also had to write my talk and practise it using the professional speaking techniques that were part of the programme.

One significant thing I'd learned was that the most powerful story you can tell is your own. I knew that I'd overcome much adversity over the years, but I didn't know how to share it in a meaningful way in just twelve minutes.

One friend suggested writing my question on a Post-it® note and sticking it next to my bed before I went to sleep. When I woke up in the morning, I'd have the answer. I figured it couldn't hurt, although it did sound rather whacky. My question was, 'What subject should I speak about?'

I wasn't feeling particularly tired that evening and decided to read for a few minutes. I don't remember what I was reading but I remember feeling slightly distracted and lifting my head from the book to look around my room. I had the clear thought that the clues to my story had to be all around me.

As I looked more closely, I noticed the felt hearts hanging across the end of my bed. I smiled, remembering how much I loved them. I had bought them when visiting some good friends who were now very much my Aussie family. As I continued looking, I saw next to my pillow another hanging heart made up of small silver bells. It occurred to me how much I loved hearts. Then I noticed the to-do list I'd written on my whiteboard; I'd drawn hearts instead of dots.

It hadn't even been fifteen minutes since I wrote my Post-it® note question. I found myself lighting up when I connected the dots and realised that my topic had to have something to do with hearts. Hearts were everywhere in my apartment: on my clothes, my jewellery, even on my fridge magnets.

I was certain that if the most powerful story I had to tell was my own, then the journey I'd be sharing had to be about my own heart. My heart felt alive. I knew I was close to getting the answer to my question; I could feel it. I followed my intuition, grabbed a notepad and scribbled down the word 'heart'. What had I learned about my own journey that I could express as lessons from my heart? As I looked back, I realised that when I had been lost after my marriage ended, it was by following my heart that I had found myself. When I thought a little deeper about what that meant, everything became clear.

I had taken five key steps to transform my life; the hearts all around me had been guiding me all along. Just twenty-five minutes after I'd written the Post-it® note question, I had my answer. I hadn't even managed to turn off the light.

Hope, Energy, Action, Resilience and Trust – H.E.A.R.T.® – five steps that took me from lost to found and revealed my power to make change happen.

H.E.A.R.T. helped me heal after heartbreak and find the courage to start a new life in Australia. I didn't realise then that I would be leaning for a second time on this same method when I eventually left my corporate career.

I share more of the method and my personal journey in the following chapters, but here is a quick overview to give you a sense of its power.

I use the metaphor of a car journey to explain this method as I go through each step. I've found it useful and the simplest way to describe how it works and how it can be leveraged.

One of the many things I've learned about myself over these last few years is that I'm great at simplifying things. I used to think it was because it was the only way my brain could take things in. This is perfectly true, but I also know it is an awesome skill to have. I used to believe that people who made things sound complex were more intelligent than me. Now I appreciate that I actually have a great skill in being able to take people on a journey with me. After all, real intelligence is about helping other people, not making yourself look good. Kudos to keeping things simple.

The H.E.A.R.T.® self-leadership method

People often say 'follow your heart', but are rarely able to explain how. If you are going to be an Unstoppable

Woman, then following this practical self-leadership method will help you do exactly that. I anchored the method in self-leadership because until you know how to lead yourself, you're not going to be able to lead others effectively. That's goes for leadership both at work and home – after all, this is life leadership.

H.E.A.R.T.® Self Leadership Method© Heart of Human

Step 1: HOPE
How Our Purpose Evolves

You might have heard the quote by Lewis Carroll, 'If you don't know where you are going, any road will get you there.' I like this quote because it tells us clearly that spending time agonising over choices and decisions when you don't know where you are going is rather pointless. You might as well choose any path because it will take you somewhere. If you don't know where you want to go, then what does it matter where it leads you?

But, if you want to live a life you love, but haven't defined what that life looks like, then you'll never know which path is best suited. You might even fail to recognise it when you stumble across it. The same goes for success. If you don't know what it looks like, or how to measure it, how can you tell when you have it?

This first step – Hope – assures that your purpose will evolve over time, and also acknowledges that we must have a chosen direction to begin with, a north star that we seek to move towards.

Successful self-leadership requires knowing where you want to go. Hope focuses on identifying your destination, determining how to get there and affirming your inner belief to move towards it.

Hope is your inner GPS – it guides you to what your heart really wants. In a more practical sense, you can view GPS as your 'Goals, Pathways & Self-Belief' for the journey ahead.

I help you become clear on how to set goals that are in alignment with you achieving heart and mind coherence so that you aren't left feeling torn between the two.

Step 2: ENERGY
Enthusiasm Not Effort
Resourcefully Grows You

We know that cars require fuel to get you to your destination. While setting your inner GPS is necessary, you also need to consider whether you have enough fuel to get there.

I used to believe that effort was the fuel we needed for the journey ahead. But I've learned over these last few years that enthusiasm is a significantly more sustainable option. Think of effort as fossil fuel and enthusiasm as renewable energy.

Learning how to acquire the right fuel and having a sustainable source of energy makes it a significantly less challenging journey to embark on.

You learn that your tank needs four types of fuel – Physical, Emotional, Mental and Spiritual. It takes more than just a strong mindset to reach the destination you have chosen.

I help you understand how to optimise your fuel to be more efficient and how to become more aware of whose tank you are filling. If you wish to reach your destination, you need to know how to fill your own tank first. Only give fuel to others from your overflow to make sure that your tank never runs empty.

Step 3: ACTION
Always **C**ontinue **T**o **I**gnite **O**utcomes **N**ow

There is no point in setting your GPS and filling your tank if you aren't prepared to press the ignition, release the handbrake and put your foot on the accelerator. Ideally with the car facing in the direction you want to travel.

You've probably already tried to drive with your handbrake on. Have you ever noticed how fear, procrastination and inertia prevent you from moving forward and achieving the outcomes you want? Well they are your handbrake.

I show you how to develop your own personal system to overcome fears and procrastination so that you can ignite the outcomes you want for your life.

Please don't take my word for it. You will be doing most of the work and will see for yourself.

Step 4: RESILIENCE
Recognise Every Season In Life Is
Evolution Not Certain Extinction

One thing I know about life is that there are always set-backs and obstacles along the way. It's inevitable.

Consider this step as the evolution of your purpose and allow your GPS to recalculate as necessary to find an alternative route to your eventual destination. You will learn how to recover quickly and consistently and stay the course to achieve what your heart wants: you become unstoppable.

My biggest growth came from adversity; it's likely yours will too, or already has. Many of us feel we want to give up at some point. I know I did when the journey got too difficult. I wish someone had shown me how to keep my mind clear and my heart aligned to finding alternative paths to my destination. I would have been much more aware of what was happening in my life. With this insight I wouldn't have felt the same embarrassment or shame each time I failed. I would certainly have been further along my journey if I'd been given the tools to master resilience and recognise that resilience wasn't simply getting back up after a setback.

I sometimes wonder if had to learn these lessons the hard way so that I could simplify them and show you how to avoid the potholes that I continually drove into.

Step 5: TRUST
Truth **R**eveals **U**niversal **S**trength **T**oday

Trust is like driving in the dark with the headlights illuminating just enough of the road in front of you. You can't see much of the road ahead, but you trust that as long as you keep moving forward, the road to your eventual destination will be lit up.

I want to show you how to cultivate an unstoppable inner confidence that enhances your impact and influence. I want to show you how to get comfortable with uncertainty and begin to trust in yourself, in others and in the journey ahead, especially when you can't know for certain that you will reach your destination.

There is strength in revealing truth. I share mine so that you can see that trust is a core foundation for cultivating inner confidence. Once you master this, you'll be well on your path to your heart's desire.

Now that you know the steps to uncovering the power of your heart, I will take you through each step of my journey so that you can use them on your own journey.

TWO

Hope
How Our Purpose Evolves

Never lose hope, my dear heart,
for miracles dwell in the invisible.
Rumi

Bigger than a four-letter word

When I think about hope, there's so much this small four-letter word conjures up.

My first memory of hope was when I was around three years old. I was standing on the sofa looking out of the window, hoping for my dad to come home. I watched the red cars go past, left to right, right to left; none of them were my dad's. I waited and waited and waited some more. I spent what felt like the whole day there waiting.

39

My mum got cross with me, telling me to move away from the window because he wasn't going to come. I didn't understand. Why would he not be coming to get me?

What I hadn't comprehended at that time was that my parents had separated, and my dad hadn't been around for months. His visits were sporadic; despite the communication to my mum that he'd be coming that day, he didn't show up.

As a three-year-old, my hope was the belief that he would come. My hope was unwavering; even though my mum told my three-year-old self several times that day that he wasn't going to come. I should move away from the window. As the hours went by, I continued believing. I still had hope.

Only that day, Mum was right, and I was left feeling disappointed and confused.

Each of us have moments from our childhood that shape who we become as adults. As a three-year-old, my hope took a big hit that day. However, as time went by, I learned a lot about hope from my mum. I didn't realise how much I'd need those lessons until I took another big hit. This time as an adult, when my own marriage ended; I needed to lean into hope to move myself from the darkness into the light.

What is hope?

I'd never consciously thought about hope when I was growing up. I believe I understood what it was without anyone having to explain it to me. I think every human on this planet understands hope. Whether consciously or unconsciously every human connects to hope.

Hope can be many things. It can be the window into the future we seek; it can be the place where our dreams begin; it can be the voice of our purpose. Hope is a powerful motivator and a catalyst for change. It's available to every single human who wants to choose to acknowledge it. Hope isn't just an emotion or a feeling of positivity; it's much more than that. Hope merges our desires with our self-belief. Many people confuse hope for a passive emotion, but that would be a mistake as it means they misunderstand the true impact of this four-letter word.

Martin Luther King said, 'We must accept finite disappointment, but never lose infinite hope.' This statement is worth remembering as it reveals the true power of hope. Hope is infinite; it can withstand short-term disappointment, provided the hope is rooted in a better future.

Where does hope come from?

The truth is I don't know. Based on everything that I've read, there are varying opinions: some claim that it's innate in humans, or that it's something we choose, or that it comes from faith.

My personal belief is that it's a mixture of all these. As humans I believe we are born with hope, but it is also something we need to consciously choose so that we can experience its power. I believe that hope requires a deep-rooted inner belief, a faith in something much greater than yourself. Why? Because I haven't met a single person who doesn't believe they lack in some area, or are unfulfilled. A faith in something greater gives us access to dreams and to a life of higher purpose which we cannot achieve on our own.

Any situation involving hope means there is no certainty in the outcome. When you are certain about a particular outcome you have absolute knowing. That is not hope.

Hope is what we choose in the absence of knowing. Hope is anchored in faith as it requires belief. It is also usually established in a love for something, a deeper desire for a future that is better or more than what you have now.

When hope is missing

An absence of hope leads to feelings of despair. Hope-lessness can feel overwhelmingly heavy, like dark oppressive storm clouds that make it hard to believe the sky was ever clear and blue. When hope is missing it causes misery; our optimism for the future erodes and pessimism grows. The loss of hope can be crippling.

I know that many people view hope as something weak; they see it as the expectation of a future based on desire and wishful thinking. A word that implies a lack of control or agency to take personal responsibility for creating this future. But I don't see hope as a weak word – I regard it as one that's misunderstood. It is only through our hopes for our future that visions are ignited, and it is through these visions that our plans are developed. There can be no vision without hope and therefore no plan without a vision.

Whether it's on a personal level or a business level, we need hope to spark our visions and develop the plans we want to bring to life. Hope is an incredibly powerful word, even more so when you consider what it can do for us.

What hope can do for us

Hope energises us into taking hold of the life we seek, no matter how long it might take. It helps us find a way to make our dreams a reality. It also supports us through any disappointments that we face, challenging us to evolve our vision so that we continue forward on our path.

Hope helps us maintain our optimism, but don't confuse this with being optimistic. Hope goes much deeper because it understands our truest life intentions, our desires and who we want to be. Hope keeps possibilities alive; it doesn't limit our life based on our current circumstances. It shows us that more is always available to us if we allow ourselves to feel the emotion of possibility. It creates a vision for the life that we desire and gives us the belief to move towards.

Nelson Mandela said, 'I'm not an optimist, but I am a great believer of hope.' If ever there was someone who epitomised the power of hope it was him.

The essential components of hope

Hope is your inner GPS, guiding you to a better future. The three components that make up your inner GPS can help you understand how to leverage the power of hope in the most effective way. If you've been inspired by certain people and wondered how they've kept their hope alive, this is how.

GPS usually stands for 'global positioning system'. We use it every day in our cars and on our phones. It helps us locate where we are and identify where we want to go. Hope's GPS is not too dissimilar; it guides our inner selves. In this case GPS represents 'Goals, Pathways & Self-Belief', the three core components of hope.

I'm all for simple models to follow, but the steps to achieving your hope aren't easy. If you are serious about the impact you want to make in your life and be unstoppable, then this will help anchor what you need to do.

Setting your inner GPS

Goals

It begins with knowing where you want to go. When we are disconnected from our hearts we can easily get caught up with following where others go or where they tell us to go. We must regularly stop and ask ourselves where *we* want to go.

Sometimes it's not that easy. I've met plenty of people over the years and through my coaching work that don't know where they want to go or what they want to do. Full disclosure again – once upon a time that was me. We often build our lives and careers based on society and our upbringing. It's easy to go down a path that others have led you to, without questioning whether it's the one that you want or whether it makes you happy.

Gallup research, based on nearly two decades of data, tells us that (between 2000 and 2018) on average, only 30% of people have been engaged at work,[6] meaning that 70% of people have been disengaged at work.

---

6   https://news.gallup.com/poll/241649/employee-
     engagement-rise.aspx

This shows how many people don't choose goals and pathways that are aligned with their hearts. Somehow, they've got stuck; for many it's easier to remain stuck than do anything about it.

I know when I first got into my career in finance it was for two reasons:

1. Because of the security that being an accountant offered (also for anyone with an Indian cultural upbringing, you know that choosing a respectable profession is part of the expectation).

2. I chose finance because I was once told I was good at maths. This second reason is rather questionable. If anyone actually cared to challenge me on my mental arithmetic today, it wouldn't stand up to close scrutiny. But I can certainly use a calculator as well as the next person. A better reason for choosing this path would have been my natural disposition for logic, simplifying and making sense of things.

What was interesting about choosing a 'secure' career was that, despite being good at my job, I couldn't find the underlying heart connection to this path. I was certainly good at what I did, and I had a really successful career in finance by all measures – business results, financial remuneration, seniority in the businesses I worked in, international experience with well-known global brands – but I always felt an underlying niggle.

I often wondered what else I might have done if I had the chance to choose again. I loved live music, mainly acoustic guitar with singer/songwriters. I loved deep and meaningful conversations with people – I was always curious to know other people's stories about their life journeys. I loved creativity and art. Looking at this mixed bag of interests, no wonder I hadn't a clue.

My good salary, the comfortable lifestyle I'd become accustomed to and the familiar rhythm and routine of daily corporate life made it easy to stay. I enjoyed both the people I worked with and the work itself. For most of the time, it wasn't hard to ignore the inner niggle and dismiss the daydreaming of a different life as wishful thinking. I think this is what most people do; I can appreciate how easy it is to stay doing what you know. We create conditions in our lives, often through the expectations of others, and become attached to certain lifestyles that keep us stuck.

It was only when my personal life was turned upside down that I started to question the life goals I had set for myself.

We all understand and appreciate that life is precious and brief. Intuitively each of us knows that we should make more of the time we have on this earth. But the way we live often pays lip service to this truth and we find ourselves falling into the trap of accepting the life that is presented to us rather than consciously choosing the one we want.

We tell stories about our responsibilities and commitments. We justify what's stopping us with numerous excuses: we have school fees and mortgages to pay; we don't have the skills; we're too old to do something new; we lack the support of significant others; we don't have the finances to live the life we really want.

Time and time again, it's often moments of trauma that force us to pay attention. They show us that we do actually have a choice to create the life we want to live. People usually only learn how to really live when they face mortality.

My trauma moment was when my marriage ended in 2014. At that time, I didn't have the capacity for anything other than surviving the emotions I was navigating. It gave me a 'I don't give a f*ck' attitude to life and work. It was the first time in my life that I genuinely didn't give a second thought to what anyone else thought about me. I spoke my truth both at work and home, and I focused on steering my own survival from heartbreak.

The irony was that by focusing more on myself and less on other people's opinions, I probably had the best year in my job and career to date. I was on fire at work and never once felt I was pretending to be someone other than who I was on the inside – it was so liberating. It made me see how inauthentic I'd been up to that point in my career. I was always trying to please people and kept adjusting my behaviour to influence their view of me. I wanted to be respected and liked; looking back now, I see how exhausting it was.

When I started to put myself first, I began to think about the life I really wanted and the dreams I wanted to achieve. My mum reminded me of a long-held dream; one I'd had before my husband and I made the decision to start a family. A dream I'd let go.

I'd always wanted to live and work in Australia. I was lucky to be working for a global business with interests in both Sydney and Melbourne. When I say 'lucky', that's not entirely true. I'd actually chosen the organisation in 2007 because I knew it had businesses in Australia; clearly my inner GPS was tuned into what I wanted early on.

While there was no guarantee that a role would be available, I finally felt I had the courage to make it happen – this was the first time I was choosing a goal purely because I felt it would make me happy. For the first time, I wasn't chasing a role, a title, a salary – I was choosing a life. I made the decision to welcome the New Year of 2016 looking over Sydney Harbour Bridge. I had less than eleven months to make that dream a reality.

At first, I was just overwhelmed at the prospect. I'd been wanting to live and work in Australia since I first visited in 2003; there was something magical about Sydney, in particular, and the beauty of the city. Even though my last visit was in 2006 I knew it was somewhere I could still see myself living, but without any idea how to make it happen. As I hadn't managed then, what was going to be different this time?

I think the biggest difference was that I'd set a clear goal of being there by New Year's Eve. I could visualise myself there; I had genuine self-belief that I would make it happen. I guess the fact that I'd had such a strong year at work, despite suffering a miscarriage and separating from my husband, showed me that I had the necessary resilience. The fast-approaching deadline made me focus on finding the different pathways to make it happen.

Pathways

My preferred route was to transfer to Australia within my organisation, but I knew there was no guarantee of a role being available. My second option was to find a job in Australia while still in the UK; this would be tricky as I needed someone to sponsor me. The third option was to apply for a skilled visa, using my accounting qualification, quit my job and then find a job when I got out to Australia. The fourth was to take a sabbatical, enjoy travelling for a while and then network in the hope of finding a job. The fifth option was to simply book a flight and go there on holiday. While this option wasn't the same as living in Australia, it still meant I would achieve my goal of being there for New Year's Eve.

Self-Belief

What became clear to me through identifying these options, was that I had several different pathways to make my dream a reality. I had every chance of succeeding rather than a feeling that my dream was too big to realise.

Seeing the different options reduced any fear; I could see that if the first pathway failed there were still others. This stopped me feeling overwhelmed and reduced any resistance I might have because of the fear of failure. Just seeing the variety of options open to me further increased my self-belief. For the first time, I had absolute clarity that I would make it happen.

We often focus on why things won't happen rather than why they could. I'd worked with the same organisation for over eight years and never once had there been an opportunity for me to work in Australia. Yet only eight weeks later, through lots of connecting with people across my organisation and socialising (I literally told everyone I was moving to Australia), the planets aligned. I was able to interview with the general manager of one our Australian businesses, who just happened to be visiting London and looking for a Head of Finance. My focus and belief had paid off. Within six months, in June 2015, I found myself embarking on my new life in Sydney.

I know for sure I don't have super-hero powers, but I do believe the opportunity came easily because I was completely aligned with my heart and mind – we were a coherent whole. There was no resistance to what I wanted – no mixed messages, no divided energy.

Although I'd put in the work over many years for the same organisation and had a strong reputation and established credentials, I believe that by setting a clear goal, identifying the different pathways and being open to exploring new avenues, combined with the self-belief and courage to vocalise my vision and seek help from my network were what allowed me to accomplish what I hoped for. If I can do it so can you.

Tuning your inner GPS – choosing your goals

This is where you are most likely to get stuck.

Why? Because you are likely to choose a goal using the same mindset you've always had. The one that tells you that you can't have everything you want. So you do what you've always done and minimise your dreams.

If minimising isn't your issue, then your problem could be thinking really big and not knowing the pathways available, or lacking the self-belief to reach out for them.

You might also feel overwhelm when you consider what it would take to achieve such a goal, or worse, self-doubt kicks in and you begin to consider the goal too outrageous to go after. 'Who do you think you are?' mocks your inner voice, causing you to pull back before you've even started. These are all experiences I've had in the past and which I see regularly with my coaching clients.

When things feel difficult and you can't see how you will ever reach what you hope for, it's easy to allow yourself to drift. Or let yourself off the hook by convincing yourself that things will unfold exactly as they are meant to. I used to believe that if things were meant to be, they would be. I still do, but with one significant clarification – things are meant to be if *I want* and *I allow* them to be.

What I've begun to understand over the last few years is that the power of our thoughts determines our reality. We often limit the joy we can experience in our lives by believing that we can't have what we want. When we repeatedly tell ourselves this and continue to believe it, then what unfolds is a reality that is fully aligned with this belief.

Many of us live our lives passively and relinquish the inner power to create the lives we want; we leave it to fate, or worse, to others to take responsibility for our lives. We fail to recognise that we have to set our intentions, ask for what we want, harness and align our energy and let go of any resistance to receiving it.

If this doesn't resonate, think back to a time when you wanted a promotion only to then put up resistance to receiving it, with thoughts such as you aren't good enough, others are better than you, you're not convinced you can do the job, or perhaps the fear that if you were promoted you'd fail to deliver on what you committed. These are all forms of resistance. We often turn to others to validate that we are good enough and to bolster our confidence – but it's relinquishing agency to other people, rather than being masters of our own destinies.

How do you get out of your own way to get on with creating your best life?

Forget starting small: I've found it's best to start with the big life questions.

'How do you want to measure your life?' A powerful question, one that provokes deep reflection on what you really want for yourself. Another good question is, 'When you get to the end of your life, how will you know you've lived it successfully?'

Most of us acknowledge that when we think about the end of our lives, we don't want to regret the things that we didn't do, the chances we didn't take and not living to our full potential. Yet when it comes to day-to-day life, we often immerse ourselves in fears and worry about what others think of us. We rarely get on to living the truth of what we desire.

When I think about how I want to measure my life, these are the questions I ask myself:

- Did I live my truth and speak honestly from my core?

- Did I love deeply and live guided by my heart?

- Did I laugh often and heartily?

- Did I choose joy daily over fear?

- Did I choose growth and contributing over playing it safe and avoiding failure?

- Did I accept and honour who I am?

Asking the big questions allows you to understand what sparks joy in you and discover what is meaningful to your life. It helps you determine your north star. In Oprah Winfrey's words, 'You have to know what sparks the light in you, so that you in your own way, can illuminate the world.'

Tuning your inner GPS – identifying your pathways

There are many paths to lead you to your destination. The first step in finding the right path for you is to get creative. Allow yourself to think of all the possibilities without any constraint. The key is to ignore any obstacles and come up with an unedited list of all of the ways that are available for you to reach your destination.

When we let ourselves see the abundance of possibilities, not only does it enable us to stay positive, it also shows that there is always a way if we allow ourselves to be resourceful. If it helps, enrol others to brainstorm with you and let the ideas flow. I know that when I considered all my options to get to Australia, I had more optimism from seeing the different pathways. It also helped with my self-belief – knowing I had several ways to make it a reality.

It's easy to fixate on a certain path and think that's the only option. Opening up the frame makes this step significantly more powerful. You can see how many routes there are; often you can find a better route once you've had the opportunity to examine all the options.

Tuning your inner GPS –
cultivating self-belief

Without self-belief your goals and pathways will probably remain dreams that you revisit but never see yourself achieving. Hope without self-belief feels like a lost opportunity, a lack of power. You can see your goal and the pathways to it, but a lack of self-belief can result in feelings of helplessness and despair. Only when we have self-belief and take action can we go from a place of hope, to one of experience and knowing.

Where does self-belief come from and how do you get it?

The clue is in the word – self – it comes from you: it can only come from you. Although you might prefer to seek validation from others, the truth is, this is a risky path to take.

Relying on other people's belief in you gives them the power to determine your capabilities. It also relies on them having a clear and accurate perspective of you and whether they are aligned with your vision.

Consider inventors – imagine if Thomas Edison had asked his friends if they believed he could create the first commercially practical light bulb. Even if they said yes, after five hundred attempts it's likely that a few of them would be saying, 'Hey why don't you give it up, mate. Do something else?'

When you have a vision for your life, it's up to you to own that vision. The belief you need to achieve it must come from inside you. That's not to say that you won't have support from others, but it does mean that you need to anchor yourself in your own belief first. If others believe in you too, then it's a bonus.

So how do you cultivate self-belief? According to Abraham Hicks, 'A belief is only a thought I keep thinking.'[7] If you choose to 'believe' this, then you understand that

---

7   E Hicks and J Hicks, *The Vortex: Where the Law of Attraction Assembles All Cooperative Relationships* (Hay House Inc, 2009)

ultimately your belief comes from your own thoughts – the ones you think over and over again.

What thoughts do you keep thinking? Do they include, 'I can do this' or 'I can't do that'? As Henry Ford once said, 'Whether you think you can, or think you can't – you're right.'

Start taking note of your thoughts each day – are they thoughts that will help you achieve what you hope for, or are they thoughts that will hold you back? Look again at how you want to measure your life. What do you need to think over and over again to get to the end of your life and know that you lived it successfully, based on your own measures of success?

This is what happened when I started my business two years ago.

To say that our thoughts have power is an understatement. I left my corporate life with huge enthusiasm about starting my new business. I'm an all-in kinda girl so I'd dismissed the guidance I'd been given. Namely, to build my business on the side while carrying on in my corporate job so that I wouldn't feel the pressure of needing an income straightaway.

Instead of following this wise advice, I was brimming with enthusiasm and self-belief. I told myself that I'd fig- ure things out along the way. A career in finance meant

I'd done my numbers and I knew I had a runway of cash to live off while I built the business.

The reality was that the business took longer to establish than I had imagined (something others had told me, but I ignored). While I had taken care of the numbers, what I didn't account for was how my self-belief might wane from not seeing as much progress as I had hoped. The thoughts I started to tell myself were:

- 'How stupid am I to have done this.'

- 'What was I thinking leaving corporate and starting a business from a standing start.'

- 'I have no clue what I'm doing.'

- 'I'm never going to succeed.'

- 'I can't do this.'

- 'It's really hard and I can't sell to save my life.'

As you can imagine, the more I had these thoughts, the more I eroded my self-belief. I started to believe I would fail, lose my money, my home and everything I had accomplished in my life so far.

I started to think I was a failure. I was soon telling myself that I'd failed at my marriage, I'd failed at having children and now I was failing in my business. The negative thoughts spiralled fast, gaining momentum in a direction I didn't want to go. I constantly repeated these thoughts throughout the day. Instead of looking at what I was creating for the future, I looked directly at my current reality and saw myself as someone who was lost again, without a clue what to do.

Those thoughts led me to experience a severe loss of self-belief and took me down a dark path where I struggled with depression and anxiety. I talk more about what happened and how I navigated this in later chapters, but needless to say, it left me under no illusion about the power of my thoughts.

Our thoughts have significant influence. I learned the hard way how destructive my thoughts could be if I continued thinking ones that didn't serve me.

How my purpose evolved

The crucial thing to realise is that what you hope for can evolve over time. Hope is **H**ow **O**ur **P**urpose **E**volves.

While I have talked extensively about following your inner GPS, setting goals, identifying pathways and cultivating self-belief, you also have to acknowledge that your goals can change over the years.

When I was sixteen, my hope was to get married and have children. I hoped to find my soulmate by the age of eighteen, date for three years, get engaged at twenty-one and married at twenty-three. I would have my first baby at twenty-five, second at twenty-seven and third at twenty-nine. After all that, I thought I'd be living my best life raising children and living happily ever after.

Reality looked rather different. At the age of thirty I'd just got married and my hope was still to have babies. It also included a new goal to successfully navigate a career as a senior leader in finance and be an equal contributor to the household.

Today aged forty and currently living a single life with no kids, my hope is simply to be happy and live a life in alignment with my heart and to help others do the same. I still have a strong desire for a loving relationship and children of my own, which I have no doubt will happen, but my hope has evolved into finding meaning and happiness in my life every single day. I don't want my happiness to depend on conditions that haven't yet become a reality.

I've learned to remind myself of the ways I want to measure my life. These are by:

- Living my truth and speaking honestly from my core

- Loving deeply and living according to my heart

- Laughing often and heartily

- Choosing joy daily over fear

- Choosing growth and making a contribution to playing it safe and avoiding failure

- Accepting and honouring who I am

These reminders help me appreciate the journey I am taking to the destination I have set. They help me choose the pathways that I'll take, and identify the self-belief I need to cultivate to reach for what I hope will be my best life.

Summary: Know where you want to go

Successful leaders know where they want to go. Give yourself the opportunity to acknowledge your own evolution. Hope is the first step in connecting to your heart and becoming unstoppable.

When you think about hope – remember it's about connecting to your inner GPS – Goals, Pathways & Self-Belief. You don't have to worry because you won't go wrong if you follow your inner guidance system. It knows exactly where you are and where you really want to be.

Always keep at the forefront of your mind how you want to measure your life; choose the goals that are most aligned to making your heart sing. Identify all the different pathways that are available and recognise that there isn't just one route to your destination; there are many. The important thing is to keep your eyes open.

Be consistent with focusing on your self-belief. It comes from within you. Remember that thoughts impact your self-belief and your reality. Choose thoughts that serve you and eliminate ones that endorse your limitations. Notice if you are consistently siding with your limitations (saying why you *can't* do something instead of why you *can*) with yourself and others. Remember that belief is a thought you keep thinking.

Now that you know about hope, we explore energy in the next chapter and how to fuel yourself for the journey ahead. After all, if you don't have fuel you won't get far.

THREE

Energy

Enthusiasm Not Effort
Resourcefully Grows You

The only thing that can grow
is the thing you give energy to.
Ralph Waldo Emerson

By keeping my energy focused on the life that I want, rather than wasting it on what I don't want, and consistently tuning into the frequency of my desire (like tuning into a favourite radio station), then the inevitable result is the life that I've focused all my energy on.

Can you see how powerful this is? You may have heard of the Law of Attraction – attracting into your life what you focus on – and dismissed it as wishful thinking.

After the break-up of my marriage I learned a lot about energy as fuel for the life I wanted. While I was heartbroken about the end of the relationship, I remained focused on creating the life I wanted. I was determined not to remain stuck looking backwards, wasting time wishing that things could be different. I didn't want my attention to be on the things I no longer had, magnifying the fact that the life I was living didn't match the one I'd envisaged.

I recognised that to move forward I needed to fill my tank with the right energy for where I wanted to go. My focus on Australia was a great anchor for my energy and attention. It was something that excited me; by directing my focus on creating the life I wanted and channelling all my attention on it, I ultimately made it happen.

During that period of my life, sadness was frequently draining my energy, but I recognised that I needed to find ways to keep my energy up. I knew that my energy could be altered by the power of my thoughts and I con-centrated on training my thoughts to stay positive. I used a variety of methods which I share in this chapter.

It's important to acknowledge, however, that the focus following the end of my marriage was solely on cre-ating a new life in Australia. What I learned from subsequent challenges was that this focus needs to be consciously maintained. The downward spiral I experi-enced when I started my business happened because I failed to consistently apply my own method. I learned that the H.E.A.R.T.° self-leadership method, while easy to understand, isn't a simple 'set and forget'. It's for life – it requires consistent and conscious application.

In this chapter I share two core principles about energy which will be your foundation for managing your own energy. I also describe the four types of fuel you need to fill your tank. But before I do, I want to explain what it means when your tank is empty.

Running on empty

To continue the metaphor of a car journey – how far do you think your car can go on an empty tank?

Not far, right?

No doubt it's something you have already experienced in your own car; you may even have tested it, driving that little bit further when the warning light comes on. I've done it a few times, and it's a horrible feeling never quite knowing if I'm going to make it to the next fuel station. The stress and fear of running out of fuel sends my heart and my mind racing.

When it comes to our own energy levels, I know we don't have a fuel gauge displayed on a dashboard in our bodies. We can't actually see how much fuel is left in our tanks, but we all know the difference between what a full tank feels like and one that feels drained. We experience the same stress that running low on fuel brings. But for some reason, we still attempt to function on empty – why is that?

If we try to avoid it with our cars, why don't we do the same with our bodies?

When most people think about energy, they focus on the energy they need to get things done, wanting more energy to do more. How often do people who seek more energy ask themselves, 'Who do I want to be and where do I want to go?'

Making sure you have a full tank to drive your car matters when you are going somewhere. It's even more important when you are going somewhere you have consciously chosen: a destination that aligns with where you want to be.

Many of us get caught up building our energy levels without questioning whether the fuel is for a clear destination, one we actually want to visit. Often, we find ourselves consuming fuel driving towards someone else's choice of destination.

How much time and energy have you wasted heading towards someone else's destination? Perhaps you thought you were filling your own tank, when you were actually filling up someone else's, without even realising that your own tank was still empty.

Your level of energy and whether you are actually filling your own tank, or someone else's, will tell you whether the destination you've chosen is aligned with what you want and who you want to be. Consider this energy step a sense check for you on the goals and pathways you have chosen.

If you lack energy or aren't filling your own fuel tank, then ask yourself if the destination you are heading towards aligns with where you want to go and inspires you to be the person you want to be.

This quote by Epictetus is worth remembering, 'First say to yourself what would you be; and then do what you have to do.' It's a message in getting focused. When you decide who you want to be and understand what this involves, you become more discerning about the choices you make and where you invest your energy.

Many people are afflicted with the disease to please, saying yes to things when they want to say no. The impact of this is that they experience the effects of their own intentions. What I mean by this is that you detract energy and time from the things that you actually love doing due to your intention (conscious or unconscious) to be liked or accepted by others. Alternatively, if the disease to please doesn't apply to you, you might be someone who thinks you should do everything yourself. This intention (conscious or unconscious) stops you from accepting and receiving help from others.

If you pay close attention to your intentions, you can see the effects of them on your life and your energy levels. The intention of wanting to be liked means you always choose to do things that please others more than yourself. The intention of thinking you can always do things better yourself, rather than accepting others' help, limits your growth and the opportunity to expand your impact.

Both are sure ways to drain your energy tank.

Perhaps you are one of those wonderfully compassionate people who always gives to others and puts yourself last. If you are a parent, I can imagine how easy it is to put yourself last, behind your family. As generous and compassionate as this might be, please stop. Don't give to anyone, including your family, if you are attempting to run on empty.

We've all heard the safety talk on planes, telling us to put on our own oxygen masks first before attending to others – there is a reason for this. We are no good to anyone if we can't breathe ourselves.

You can't be unstoppable if you empty your fuel tank for everyone else's benefit.

Filling up your own tank first and then giving others fuel from your overflow is not a selfish thing to do. It is incredibly generous. When you are full, the abundance of life within you flows out to others around you. When you feel vibrant, energetic, alive inside – how can others not benefit? Having a full tank means that you have more to give, not less.

Burnout was something I was never aware of when I was growing up; today I hear the word everywhere. I know fear has a huge role to play. Our drive to impress, to seek validation, to prove we are worthy, that we are good enough, generates behaviours that don't serve us. We work harder and longer to prove our worth, putting ourselves last. This ultimately leads to burnout.

One thing I learned from corporate life is that you can give more and more and more; no-one ever tells you to stop. Some kind soul might say, 'Hey you're working too hard, give yourself a break.' The reality is that most of these people are doing exactly the same or else you think that they are not important enough for you to pay attention to them.

If you are looking for a pat on the back for working your ass off and seeking a huge round of applause from the people you do it for, forget it. Validation of your own worth has to come from you.

When you set your intention to be your true self and only do what is in alignment with your heart, you begin to ask questions such as, 'Does saying yes to this move me closer to what and who I want to be and where I want to go?'

When you act with the intent of being your true self, you learn to say no to the things that don't align with you. You conserve your fuel for the destination you have chosen.

If you're unsure what your true self is, ask yourself, 'When do I feel most alive?' That's what your life and being your true self are really about.

Before you can start regulating your energy, you need to know who you are and what is your truest intention. Then you know exactly what you want and can prioritise how you manage your energy to reach the destination you have set. Let's look at the two foundation principles of energy.

Principle 1 – Enthusiasm over effort

Most people subscribe to the principle that if you want to achieve more in life you need to do more. As a consequence, more and more of us experience exhaustion and burnout.

The biggest mistake you can make in trying to achieve more, is by applying more effort. What most of us fail to realise is that the problem isn't the volume of activity or the time we spend on it, it's the fact we need effort to do it in the first place.

Effort, by its very meaning, requires 'extra energy' to do something. When you make the effort to do anything, it requires using more force or energy than would otherwise be necessary. The word itself implies difficulty, a bit of grind, a slog.

On the other hand, when you consider the word enthusiasm – what feelings does it arouse? Eagerness? Excitement? Interest? Enjoyment? Fun?

If you are enthusiastic about what you are doing, think how much more you would achieve. And what exactly would it feel like? I know when I'm enthusiastic about something, I'm excited. I can't wait to start and get stuck in. I often find I can go for hours without checking the time and I still have an abundance of energy to continue. That's how I feel writing this book. When I am enthusiastic, I feel unstoppable.

What's fascinating is that I've never heard of anyone experiencing burnout from an overdose of enthusiasm. Unfortunately, I can't say the same for effort. The challenge is that we have social and work cultures that reward effort, not enthusiasm. We have jobs where we have to do certain things that we are not enthusiastic about. People equate leadership with hard work and effort, but with the increasing mental stress we are constantly under, it's time for that paradigm to shift.

We are currently in the 'imagination age', or as some describe it, the fourth industrial revolution. We need to leverage imagination and creativity to stay innovative and connected to people's needs. The work ethic of the industrial age is no longer suitable. Creativity is certainly not inspired by effort, and in an increasingly connected world where the boundaries between work and home life continue to blur, it's vital to harness your energy effectively.

Apart from increased energy and vitality for life, the advantage of enthusiasm over effort is the fact that nothing feels like work. You have more time because enthusiasm drives greater productivity and efficiency. You feel happier, experience more enjoyment and feel more aligned and in tune with yourself. You get to do more of what you love, find more inspiration and ultimately feel unstoppable.

Of course, there are downsides. With more energy generated by your enthusiasm, to pursue what you want, you are bound to be in demand. However, some people might want to keep you in the 'effort game' because they find your enthusiasm too much and are unnerved by it. You could also become the object of jealousy and envy by those who want the same freedom you've found. Ultimately, the biggest downside is that you no longer have any excuse for not getting things done. OK, these are hardly downsides, but I genuinely can't think of any real downsides.

Perhaps you have doubts and thoughts that hold you back – keeping you in the same effort game you've always played. You might think it's impossible to opt for enthusiasm each day in your home and work lives. You continue to believe that effort is necessary. You also defend your limitations and give excuses for why you can't always find enthusiasm for what you want. You accept that feeling exhausted and lacking energy are just part of day-to-day life.

I'm not writing this to change your mind; that would be too much effort on my part. I'm going to enthusiastically continue with all the other inspiring things I plan to do. I can show you through the stories I share in this book and the transformation of my life that it really does work.

In the words of Abraham Hicks, '... words don't teach. It's only life experience that teaches.'[8] Allow yourself to give it a go. Choose to do things that inspire you and discover how enthusiasm can transform your life.

The title of this chapter reminds you that **E**nthusiasm **N**ot **E**ffort **R**esourcefully **G**rows **Y**ou.

Here's a formula – OK, you can't take the finance girl out of me. It might help you when you find yourself getting stuck:

$$Energy = \frac{Enthusiasm + Inspiration}{Effort}$$

---

8   A Hicks, 'Achieving momentum', https://innerfreedomsystem.com/achieving-momentum/

This quote by Ralph Waldo Emerson sums it up nicely, 'Enthusiasm is the mother of effort, and without it nothing great was ever achieved.'

Principle 2 –
Comparison as a guide to joy

You may have heard the quote often attributed to Theodore Roosevelt, 'Comparison is the thief of joy.' When we compare ourselves to others, we feel bad about what we don't have, and ultimately it steals our joy and drains our energy.

However, I'd like to challenge that meaning. Comparison isn't the thief of joy: comparison is a guide to joy.

Why comparison can be a good thing

Let me explain. We rarely feel bad when we compare ourselves to people who do things or have things we don't actually want for ourselves or care about. For example, if you're not an actor, Laura Dern winning an Oscar won't upset you.

Usually, we only feel bad when we compare ourselves to someone who has something we want for ourselves. Comparison isn't stealing our joy – it points us in the direction of what we really want and where we believe our joy lies. When we can't help but compare ourselves in a negative way, what is actually being revealed is how disconnected we are to ourselves.

You will have heard the saying, 'It is not until you are lost that you begin to find yourself.' If you think about it, comparison can actually help us find ourselves.

I used to compare myself to others and believe I wasn't good enough. I'd look at my friends or colleagues and think they possessed some gift or superpower that I didn't have. I would see people I deemed to be successful and feel more and more inferior.

When I looked at others, I could see everything that I wanted for myself. The problem was that I was directing focus and energy to what I didn't have or believed I couldn't have. I wanted more for myself; I knew it was available because other people had it.

What comparison revealed to me was the disconnection to my inner self. I didn't see the truth of who I was at heart; this feeling of discomfort showed me that I didn't see myself clearly. Instead of using comparison to find out who I was, I used it to prove who I didn't think I was – which shows how separated I was from my inner self.

Instead of using comparison to guide me towards what I desired, I used it to look in the opposite direction and focus on all the things I lacked. Instead of seeing my desires as something wonderful to be embraced and to guide the journey ahead, all I could see was the distance between my life and where I really wanted it to be.

When I understood that the disconnection to my inner self was being revealed through comparison, everything shifted. I realised that when you compare yourself to others and don't view it as a guide to finding joy, that's when you feel bad. I was looking at comparison as something that was stealing my happiness instead of seeing it as a guide to joy.

Using comparison to find joy

I found that comparison was presenting me with confident people – ones who were having lots of fun, not taking themselves too seriously and living a great life. I've heard people say that you only see in others what you have within yourself; otherwise, you wouldn't recognise it. I have to say it's true – I'm confident and have fun when fully connected to my inner self.

I recognised that I was always being guided to my joy through comparison. I just hadn't understood it. I began to notice the times when I admired others but didn't compare myself to them. They showed me that I was in full alignment with myself and not separate from my inner self or seeking to be anything different.

What I've learned is that comparison and contrast aren't things we need to hide from. Nor can we hide from them.

We now have the entire planet to compare ourselves to: we constantly check Instagram and Facebook, examining the lives of other people. It usually leaves you feeling inadequate.

What is helpful in these social media-soaked times is to embrace the awareness that comparison can give us, revealing where we have become disconnected to ourselves. When we are fully connected to ourselves, instead of feeling jealous or incompetent, what we feel for other people are happiness, joy, excitement and enthusiasm.

When we're disconnected from ourselves that's when we notice that looking at other people shows us what's lacking within us. The truth is we are really seeking connection to ourselves and the feeling of joy when we are in full alignment. That's when we feel satisfaction and harmony in our lives.

Comparison is an opportunity to check our alignment to ourselves. Instead of feeling bad, we can use it as a guide to joy.

Compare yourself to others, then take action

When you are in comparison mode, what do you notice it reveals about what you want? Pay close attention to how you feel. Make a conscious choice to feel good because comparison is reminding you to connect to yourself.

Try this quick exercise. If you notice you're comparing yourself to someone and it's not making you feel great, say to yourself, 'This is telling me to pay attention to something that I want which remains unfulfilled in my life.'

Start noticing what your comparison reveals about what you really desire; be grateful for the guidance it provides in your own quest for joy. As you become aware of your desires being similar to those of your peers or people in your social media feeds, acknowledge each little win and other signs that indicate you are moving in the right direction.

Rejecting comparison as the 'thief of joy'

You might not agree with what I'm saying, but please indulge me and consider the following. If you continue to view comparison as the thief of joy, acknowledge that you are choosing to feel unworthy, not good enough and thereby limiting your potential. Ultimately, you become paralysed by these negative attitudes. They will stifle any potential to live a rich and joyful life.

On the flip side, by using comparison as a guide to what makes you feel happy, you choose fulfilment, clarity, enthusiasm, enrichment, freedom, connection to yourself, connection with others and a life full of joy and satisfaction.

Are you going to opt to think what you've always thought? Feel what you've always felt? Say what you've always said? Or are you going to choose joy to maintain your energy levels and take appropriate action to achieve your personal goals?

The choice is always yours: you can either choose dissatisfaction and being dragged down by comparison, or freedom from all of this. Comparison is not a thief; it's a guide to your joy. The decisions you have to make are how you view it and what you choose.

It's time to explore the types of energy you require for your journey.

Four energy types

To proceed towards your destination, you need four different types of energy or fuel: emotional, mental, physical and spiritual.

As you continue to discover how enthusiasm – not effort – resourcefully grows you, and how you can use comparison to guide you towards your joy, you'll see that these principles require both emotional and mental energy to fuel your tank.

1. Emotional energy

What role it plays

When your emotional energy is in balance, you are more empathetic and inclusive, more open to other people and new situations. You find that you are less judgemental and show greater compassion and generosity in all of your relationships and interactions both at work and at home.

Paying close attention to your feelings is the fastest way to work out whether you brim with emotional energy or are depleted. When you are full of emotional energy you feel good. Your interpretation of the world around you is positive and you enjoy healthy relationships.

By zoning out distractions and tuning into your feelings, you are better able to monitor your inner core. Your feelings are always the first indicator of whether you are in alignment with what you want: it's important to pay attention to them.

How to find your emotional fuel

What I've learned about emotional energy is that to keep my level high, I have to choose to care how I feel and make it a priority every day.

Notice the stories: Raising this awareness helped me to see how often I chose to tell stories about my circumstances that actually made me feel worse and depleted my energy levels.

When I was healing from my marriage ending, I kept a journal. Each day I wrote two stories. The first was my old story – the one I woke up with and didn't want; the second was my new story – the one I wanted to create.

Writing my old story helped me purge the unhappy thoughts from my mind and get rid of any negative energy trapped in my body. It showed me the unhelpful narrative that was running on a loop through my mind. The habit of writing a new story every day did wonders for my mindset and energy levels.

Have you ever noticed how your energy changes based on the stories you tell yourself? I saw how disempowering my old stories were and how they could keep me trapped in the past. My new stories were creative, inspiring and limitless in their reach. They helped me believe in the possibility of achieving my dreams. The more work I did on managing my energy, the more dynamic I felt. It propelled me towards the future I wanted.

When I left my corporate career, I'd forgotten this practice of writing stories to sustain my energy. We all know someone who talks constantly about all the things that are going wrong and feels that life has given them a raw deal. I'm quite sure that was me a couple of years ago.

Choose your feelings: Everything has its opposite. Feelings are no different. When we are sad, we know that the opposite is being happy. But it's not always possible to choose to switch from feeling sad to happy; it doesn't ring true. But when you consciously acknowledge that you don't want to feel sad, you can replace it with the next best feeling and start to create a habit of choosing that feeling instead.

Instead of focusing on what's causing the sadness and trying to feel better about it, opt to think about a different part of your life, one that you already feel good about and which gives you easy access to a better feeling. When we feel better, we live better.

Pay attention to body signals: Another way to increase your emotional energy is by noticing what signals your body gives in a particular situation. When your body doesn't give you the signal that indicates a resounding 'Hell, yes', then stop and pay attention to any doubts you might have. The doubts usually mean you shouldn't do it: they could be warning you that you are headed in completely the wrong direction.

Your inner GPS tells whether you are acting in alignment with your truest self. The feelings in your body give you clues long before your thoughts and brain catch up. Re-centre yourself and become still for a while before making any big decisions. When every cell in your body gives you a resounding 'yes' – then move forward.

Set clear boundaries: How good are you at setting boundaries? Do you say yes when you mean no? Do you overgive to others? Start to protect your time; it's your life. How you spend your time defines your life. Each day represents your life in miniature and is a fresh opportunity to put your time to better effect. Don't let people who are like vampires suck your time and energy away; don't let others rob you of the light within you.

Protect yourself fiercely by setting boundaries and sticking to them. A lack of clear boundaries gives others the freedom to take advantage of your good nature. If you are wasting time, ultimately you are wasting your life. We all know how it feels after being with someone who drains your energy; if it doesn't feel good – limit your time with them.

I like the saying, 'Fill your own cup first and then let others only drink from the overflow, that way your cup is never empty.' Put yourself first so that you are better placed to give to others. Remember that you can't give to others what you don't have; everyone loses when you are empty. Also, when you give to everybody else and never to yourself, you are confirming to yourself that 'I have a life that I don't believe I'm worthy of living.' What's the point of being alive, if not to feel alive yourself?

Do what nourishes you and makes you feel good, whether that's reading a good book, having a soak in the bath, catching up with a friend, meditating or writing a gratitude journal. Do it for yourself, to fill your energy reservoir.

2. Mental energy

What role it plays

Your mental energy impacts your thoughts, attitudes and judgement – about both yourself and others. When your mental energy is aligned, your thoughts are positive, you have an open attitude and you are more proactive. Your problem-solving skills improve. You demonstrate more focus and a clarity of mind that allows you to communicate with others more effectively. You are less judgemental and are more open to seeing and hearing alternative perspectives.

How to find your mental fuel

Get present and breathe: The best way to fuel yourself mentally is by slowing down your thoughts and creating space in your mind to allow for clarity about what you want to surface. Focus on your breath and be present in the moment; after all it's the only one you exist in. Release any tension by letting your breath be your anchor. Inhale slowly and exhale slowly; let go of anything you cannot control. Let go of thoughts and focus on what's right in front of you. It's easy to let your energy be depleted by things you can't control; being mindful allows you to remain focused on what you can.

Change your thoughts: Become aware of recurring thoughts and begin to discard them from your life. Say good riddance to thoughts that don't support your self-care, self-esteem and self-worth. Look out for any narratives you keep repeating – do they support you to feel good or not? If not, replace them with thoughts that are kinder to you. Talk to yourself as if you were talking to your best friend; begin to sense the shift you feel in your own wellbeing and how your confidence increases.

Make room for the right people: Say goodbye to, or limit time with, people who discourage your growth, drain your energy and don't support you. This can be tough, but acknowledge that you and your life are valuable commodities; if there are people who don't appreciate your value, let them go and allow the ones who do to take their place. You have to make room for what you want by letting go of what you don't.

Press reset: Stop repeating patterns that don't serve you. Get rid of the things in your home that don't bring you joy or serve any useful purpose. Ultimately, remove anything that doesn't enhance the best of you. Give yourself some tough love and press the reset button as often as you need to; start afresh each morning and over a few days and weeks you will see how the world around you shifts.

Choose an attitude of possibility: Remember that your attitude is everything to do with what you receive from others and give to others – choose an attitude of possibility not one of resignation. When the chatter in your mind hampers and drains you, use meditation to clear your head and make space for calming, helpful thoughts. I never understood how meditation would help me until I made it part of my daily practice. Now I realise how necessary meditation is to access my inner wisdom to always find a way.

Our thoughts become our reality – choose wisely.

3. Physical energy

What role it plays

Your body usually tells you when things are not well and it is obvious to you and others when it is drained of energy. Physical energy should be the simplest form of energy to understand and nurture, but this knowledge isn't always acted on.

You know that you need to eat healthy foods, drink more water and get regular sleep and exercise to keep your body healthy, flexible and pain free. But they are not always the easiest things to do. We have to choose to make health our priority.

How to find your physical fuel

Nurture your body: Start by making time for exercise; get up a little earlier and begin with a 30-minute daily walk. Not only will it boost your energy, it helps maintain your resolve to do the right things for yourself overall – eat more nutritious food, get adequate sleep, live a healthy life. If you believe that nurturing your body is the best investment you can make, then the return is priceless. Don't trade your health for wealth, as tempting as it is, or you end up trading your wealth for health, something that money cannot buy.

Repetition is the one of the best ways to change a habit and reinforce learning. I know that I failed myself by giving up the daily practice of consciously taking note of my energy levels. I almost let my tank drain empty.

Choose to rest: Take time to rest; we aren't 24/7 machines. Giving yourself time to just 'be' is essential to your mission on this earth. It's only through resting and recharging that we get the clarity and energy required to make the impact we want in our lives. You have a unique contribution to make. Don't lose sight of this by getting caught up in the daily grind.

Knowing is not the same as doing: There is a big difference between knowing and doing, but until you do something you don't really know it. Create space in your day for self-care and physical exercise to support your emotional and mental wellbeing. Be mindful of overcommitting yourself; choose only to say yes to things that feel good and that you feel in complete alignment with. I feel as though I've learned these lessons the hard way – I hope you won't have to.

4. Spiritual energy

What role it plays

When your tank of spiritual energy is full you have a greater connection with yourself, you are more aligned with your purpose and you have a sense of something greater than yourself. As a result of this connection and purpose you feel a sense of calmness, you are more in flow and even find that you are more creative. There is also a feeling of fearlessness. This alignment and clarity of purpose bring certainty and eliminate any doubts about achieving anything you want.

How to find your spiritual fuel

Be in alignment with who you want to be: When you decide what you most want to give to the world, letting anything that doesn't align with this intention fall away, your focus is on creating the life you want. By acknowledging the fact that if you don't act on the things that you most value, your day will be filled with other people's priorities. It's important to remember who you are, the contribution you want to make and the destination you have set for your life. Stop doing anything that doesn't directly or indirectly support you in achieving your mission and you'll see your energy multiply exponentially. You create spiritual fuel when you are connected to yourself and your sense of purpose. When any fears you have about moving in the direction you want fall away, you know that your spiritual tank is full.

Learn from others who are aligned: I hadn't really listened to many podcasts prior to 2014, but I remember the first one I listened to when I was healing from my marriage break-up. It was *Life is a Marathon* by Bruce Van Horn[9]. I learned how this wonderful, kind-hearted man had been through his own life struggles. He had survived stage four cancer and was embracing the beauty of his life and gracing the world with this gift.

I listened to Bruce's podcast every morning on my drive to work. His kindness and love lifted my energy and strengthened my hopes for a better tomorrow. I have always loved hearing other people's stories and I really enjoyed listening to his journey and following his life.

I've since added many other teachers to my podcast list, including Oprah Winfrey's *Super Soul Sessions*,[10] Jay Shetty's *On Purpose* podcast[11] and *The School of Greatness* by Lewis Howes.[12]

These are just some of the amazing resources by inspiring people that can help lift your energy, get you through challenging periods and remind you of who you are.

---

9   www.lifeisamarathon.com/author/liamwpadmin
10 www.oprah.com/own-supersoulsessions/listen-to-oprahs-supersoul-conversations-on-apple-podcasts_1
11 https://jayshetty.me/podcast
12 https://lewishowes.com/sogpodcast

Summary: Acquire the fuel for your journey

You need to keep your energy tank full. Energy isn't all about fuelling you to do more. First you have to understand who you are and what you want, so that you choose the right type of fuel to create a life in alignment with your own vision, not somebody else's.

Pay attention to your underlying intentions; the reality that you currently experience in life is linked to these intentions. Be careful of any intentions that don't serve you or your vision for your life. Get in touch with your truest intention – that of being yourself, making an impact, and living a life that makes you feel most alive.

Make a conscious decision to manage your energy and keep your own tank full: let others benefit from your overflow. Notice what makes you enthusiastic and what feels like an effort that is draining you. Where you find enthusiasm lies your source of energy. Use comparison as a guide to your joy. Keep checking your emotional, mental, physical and spiritual fuel tanks. Make sure they are full so you are always ready to embark on the next stage of the journey towards your destination.

FOUR

Action

Always Continue To Ignite
Outcomes Now

*Don't judge each day by the harvest
you reap but by the seeds that you plant.*
Robert Louis Stevenson[13]

There are two stand-out instances of great action in my life. The first was moving from England to Australia and starting a new life down under at the age of thirty-five. The second was leaving my corporate career three years later to start my own business.

In both instances the tension of standing still was too much; I needed to act. I've already talked about my move to Australia and what prompted it, so I'll share a little more about what led me to taking the leap to start my own business.

---

13   RL Stevenson, *Admiral Guinea* (A Word To The Wise, 2013)

When it came to my career, I had the privilege of working for some great global businesses. I spent ten and a half years working in my last job, working across several different companies within the group. Each area I worked in exposed different aspects of myself and my leadership. It gave me the opportunity to adapt to the different cultures within the business and allowed me to discover what I liked and didn't like.

What I learned during my time working for large corporates was that I wasn't a 'yes' person. I had opinions, points of view and I wasn't afraid to voice them. I thrived in work cultures where diversity of thinking and challenge were welcome. I enjoyed environments that were ambitious with a strong drive for exceptional performance, but were also heart- and human-centred.

I also learned that the person you work directly for has a huge bearing on your career experience. I was extremely lucky for the majority of my seventeen-year career to work with exceptional and inspiring leaders. There were, however, three leaders who stand out for a less-than-positive experience. These included both female and male leaders; the experiences involved bullying, micro-management and narcissism.

As I look back, I can see how each of these experiences had a huge impact on my confidence levels, my self-esteem and self-worth. I felt extremely isolated at times and, being a self-reflective person, I often looked inward to try and identify what might have been wrong with me. I reflected on who I needed to be to get a different result and often adapted my behaviour. Although I wasn't a 'yes' person, I didn't want to be seen as an agitator or troublemaker by speaking out. This is what often happens when you choose to stand up and be seen. I also wanted to be liked and to be respected.

The truth is corporate bullying and bad leadership are more common than most people realise. As someone who isn't a 'yes' person, I learned a lot about why people don't speak out and stand up for each other. I observed a great deal of fear in the teams I worked with over the years. I noticed that outside of meetings colleagues would discuss raising issues at team meetings and talk of standing together to bring about change. But I often ended up being the lone voice in raising perspectives that challenged the status quo. Many a time colleagues would congratulate me for raising a difficult subject and offer their support. This was usually in corridors or back at our desks, never in meetings or at a time when I needed someone to stand with me. You may have had similar experiences.

Brené Brown helped me to understand that there are plenty of people shouting their opinions and offering their support from the cheap seats, but few are willing to get into the arena with you and fight. I also learned from my own personal experience that the leaders you work for can turn you from hero to zero in no time, simply because you've had the courage to say what others are thinking but don't openly voice. It made me really aware of how much people feel the need for self-preservation within this environment, and I don't blame them. Being someone who spoke up didn't win me the popularity vote with the leaders who were insecure in themselves and used their positions of power to shore up their own sense of worth.

Being a lone voice often led me to look deeper at myself and figure out why I didn't just keep my head down. Why was I so incapable of playing office politics? Why did I care so much?

I did care; I've always cared – that's what I am passionate about and have enthusiasm for. The truth is I've no time for politics – I never have. I know and understand that bureaucracy and hierarchy keep large organisations functioning the way they do and keep people in line, but deep down I've always believed there is a better way.

I did, however, care about what people thought about me. I found it difficult during these periods of poor leadership because I didn't understand why these leaders couldn't see me clearly. I've always cared more about doing the right thing. I acknowledge that it sometimes made me unpopular, but it did make me realise something important. Some people cared about looking good; I cared more about doing good. This was always going to be a path that faced resistance.

Later I learned at my philosophy class that it is always best to 'speak the truth pleasantly than speak a pleasant untruth'. It was clear to me that many people prefer to speak pleasant untruths just to keep the peace and avoid the discomfort of healthy tension – it certainly wasn't me.

Another thing I learned about myself is that I'm not someone who gives up. Despite several challenging experiences, I stayed the course and focused on getting to the top of my professional career in finance. Being self-driven, good at what I do and extremely tenacious, I was determined to show these leaders what I was capable of.

It was going through my marriage separation that made me re-evaluate what I really wanted from my life. Who was I doing it for? What did I really want for myself? I enjoyed finance, although I preferred the commercial aspect involved in my roles considerably more than the financial accounting side of things. It was as though I was peeling back layers of an onion – it certainly made my eyes water.

I realised the reason I was striving to climb the ladder was to prove something to others and to myself – I wanted to show them and me that I was good enough. That I was somebody. I was using my job status, the security of my income, and the lifestyle it afforded to validate myself. Although I didn't want to admit it, deep down I knew it was true.

The bullying I experienced was early on in my career. I didn't realise how much it contributed to my commitment to get to the top of my profession just to prove that I was capable of it. Even though the person involved in the bullying was eventually let go from the business, my resolve remained rock solid.

The changes in my personal life triggered some deep soul-searching and I finally acknowledged the deeper truth to myself. I enjoyed my finance career, but it wasn't where my heart was. My stubbornness meant that it was only when I was offered a CFO role in another organisation that I finally came clean with myself and acknowledged that I wasn't in my heart space.

The healing journey I'd embarked on after my marriage ended helped me learn that I no longer wanted to be at the mercy of bad leadership; I wanted to do what made my heart sing. I loved people, I loved deep and mean-ingful connections and I was passionate about helping people and businesses get results. After seventeen years in finance you can tell I like measurable results.

But the results I wanted for my clients were not neces-sarily financial, although it would certainly be one of the outcomes. I wanted to help people find freedom and uncover their true self-expression. I wanted to work with honest and inspiring leaders who had heart and com-munity at the centre, and who revelled in helping each other rather than in self-interest. I wanted people to see how they could be strong in their self-leadership so that they could become better leaders both at home and at work and not be blocked by the fear of self-expression as many are. I wanted people to feel unstoppable.

What I valued most were connection and love. With my life looking nothing like I wanted, I realised that I would have to move towards the destination that my heart wanted to take me. My heart already knew what my mind and ego weren't ready to accept, but I'm glad I finally saw the light and decided to take a leap of faith for the future I hoped for.

It's not always easy being honest with yourself, but that's where you have to start. I've had several wake-up calls in my life journey, including losing my dad in a car accident when I was twenty-six years old. I realised that it was about time I started to pay attention and recognise how short my time on this earth was. The life I wanted wasn't going to create itself by default; I needed to move towards it – which is what I did.

The previous chapters on hope and energy show that each step in the H.E.A.R.T.° self-leadership method provides a sense check to see whether you've made the right choices, ones that align with your heart. The action step is no different – if you find that you are not taking any action, then your first question is whether the destination you have chosen is the one you want. If you are certain that the destination is right, but you can't move towards it, this chapter will help you understand what you need to be aware of when it comes to taking action. It also shares methods for moving off your starting blocks.

Why knowing is not enough

Knowing is not enough; we must apply.
Willing is not enough; we must do.
Johann Wolfgang von Goethe

I often tell people that they can't truly know something unless they do it. Most of us know that to be fit and healthy you must eat the right foods and exercise regularly. We know that to run a marathon we need to train – starting with small distances and then building up until our fitness and stamina reach marathon level. We know that if we want good teeth we need to brush them twice a day, every day. All of these require consistent action. We can't think ourselves into being healthy and fit humans, we can't think ourselves into being marathon runners and we certainly can't think ourselves into having good teeth. We can all tell ourselves that we know what is required, but the truth is until we do it, we don't really know it.

We don't understand what our own bodies specifically need to be nourished and we don't know how we would actually feel during the process of getting healthier – how our bodies and minds would change and how our energy levels would adjust. We don't know what our real experience of healthiness would actually be until we do it. It's far easier to think and say that we know what it would be like, than actually do it.

In the same way, simply having a map of where you want to go won't get you to your destination. You can spend a lot of time pondering the future you want and still find yourself in exactly the same place. You can refine every detail of the journey and continue to plan the pathways, research every turn you need to take, as well as visualise any obstacles you might face, but nothing replaces the experience of taking the actual journey. The gap between knowing and doing is huge. Words can't teach – the lesson is learned in the doing. It's from your experiences in life that you learn the most. Many of us read books on how to improve our wealth, how to be successful, how to be fit and healthy. I'm sure it's pretty clear that if we could read our way to success we'd all be lying next to a pool sipping cocktails.

Reading this book is a great opportunity for you to learn from my journey and the results I've got from applying the H.E.A.R.T. self-leadership method. But reading these words and hearing what I say won't make you unstoppable; you have to take action to bring this to life. If you struggle with taking action, let me help you go from zero to unstoppable.

Check you are facing the right direction

Before you dive into action, it's important to know that you are facing the right direction, the one you want to go in. Remember the car journey? If you release the handbrake, press on the accelerator, but head off in the wrong direction, you're unlikely to get where you want to go.

Action is so much easier when it is inspired and aligned with where you want to go. I'm going to labour this point because some people subscribe to the idea that doing something is better than doing nothing. I don't agree with this perspective because I believe we already do plenty. It's why we can't find the time to do the things we really want to do in our lives and why so many people are disengaged in their careers. It's also why so many of us experience the effects of burnout. We don't allow ourselves the opportunity to receive inspiration, which can only happen when you create space for inspiration to arise.

Facing in the right direction begins by reminding your-self of the destination you hope to reach and checking how inspired you feel about it. Are you feeling excited, enthusiastic, energised, raring to go? If not, identify what you do feel and pay close attention. This will give you a clue as to what to do next.

You might be thinking that it would be an adventure just to set off in any direction, and it certainly would. However, it's worth remembering that your hope is ulti-mately how your purpose evolves. Sometimes simply going in any direction can reveal what you truly want for yourself, often by showing you what you don't want.

The difference is that when you have a clearly identified destination which you are inspired to move towards, the consistent daily actions you take contribute to building momentum, accelerating your speed and ultimately leading you to be unstoppable much faster. Aimlessly roaming gives you a great opportunity to learn about yourself, but the constant slowing and changing of direction rarely builds up the momentum you need to feel unstoppable.

Inertia to momentum

Why is it that when it comes to our dreams many of us don't take any action to fulfil them?

Athletes cannot call themselves athletes without training consistently every day – one training session would not make an athlete. Nor does a single workout give me a six pack or toned thighs – disappointing but true. Fulfilling our dreams is no different. It requires consistent action every single day. You have to decide to begin. So, where do you start?

To create the impact you desire and live the life you want, you have to move from inertia to momentum. I didn't think I'd be revisiting science after leaving school, but I've learned that physics tells me a lot about psychology and motivation; it has helped me understand much more clearly what taking action requires.

Newton's First Law of Motion states that 'Objects will remain at rest or in uniform motion in a straight line and at the same velocity unless acted upon by an external force.' This is what we refer to as inertia. Unless there is a force on you to act differently, you'll either continue to do nothing or do the same as you've always done.

There are two main types of force that could influence your actions – intrinsic and extrinsic. Both can be helpful to shift you from inertia, but only one of them leads you to feeling unstoppable.

If your actions are influenced by extrinsic forces, it's likely that you are at the mercy of outside forces such as social pressure, status, seeking rewards, money, avoiding punishment. I once sought to learn the guitar because I thought it would be cool to be the person who everyone crowds around at a campfire. I soon realised that the cool status points I might earn weren't enough to keep me attending regular guitar lessons and putting in the hours of practice needed.

That's where most of us start our journey. Usually, we seek material wealth and move along a path that allows us to have all the trappings of a 'socially successful' life. We often find that extrinsic forces rarely connect us to our deepest levels of fulfilment. This is why many people find themselves working incredibly hard to reach the top of the mountain, accumulating nice things along the way, only to find they still feel empty at the top, lacking something deeper and more meaningful.

If you are influenced by intrinsic forces, you act according to what's inside you: your personal values, what you enjoy and have passion and enthusiasm for, what resonates with you at your core, along with what gives you a sense of meaning and purpose. Actions motivated by intrinsic forces are usually the things you do because they bring you joy. Nobody has to pay you to do them and it's unlikely you are looking for 'likes' and 'followers' or any other outcome other than the pure value you get from doing it. This is how I feel about my writing – I can spend hours writing without any other purpose than to enjoy the feeling of putting my thoughts to paper. It's also something I'm willing to spend years improving because it's fun. It's not difficult to see why intrinsic force has greater potential to move you from inertia to momentum and sustain action for the long term.

While external forces in the form of accountability buddies, coaches, mentors, leaders and friends can nudge us in the right direction and are often necessary, the real force we need to leverage is within us. It means we are never left feeling powerless.

It is worth knowing that it doesn't take much to get momentum started when you use an intrinsic force such as inspiration. Acknowledge your own intrinsic force by considering what you have chosen for your own hope and what fuels your energy. What action do you feel most inspired to take and what do you feel most enthusiastic about? Feelings always guide you; they indicate whether you are leveraging intrinsic or extrinsic forces.

The most valuable lesson I learned is that action influenced by intrinsic force feels great. It's usually inspired by love and a sense of connection to a higher and more meaningful purpose. It doesn't necessarily mean that the journey will be smooth, but it does mean that you are more likely to act and move forward, following where your heart guides and coping with any obstacles that might come up.

The present moment matters

It's sometimes easy to tell ourselves a story that says it's too late to go after what we want; we should have done something about it years ago. That's one of the reasons why I keep mentioning my age. And in case you missed it, I'm forty at the time of writing this book. I don't think I'm late to any party – if I am, then I'm happy to be fashionably late.

You may have heard the saying, 'The best time to plant a tree was twenty years ago and the next best time is now.' Stop arguing in favour of your limitations; don't make age – whether you are younger or older – a reason not to start something new or stop you from creating the life you want. Tomorrow is never a given. If you've ever lost anyone, I'm sure you know this already. But now is the time to shift from the theory of knowing to truly knowing something by doing and living it.

The quote at the beginning of this chapter really resonates with me, even more so because I recognise that in
today's society most of us seek instant gratification. We
want things to happen quickly, whether that's getting
pregnant the month we decide to have a baby, whether
it's getting a new home, a promotion, a pay rise, the
business growing, our teams performing well, being able
to play the guitar, having a book published or finding
our life partners. We want what will make us happy – we
want it now.

But it's the present moment that matters; we need to
direct our focus to what is happening right now. The
results will flow from what you choose to spend your
time on today.

Robert Louis Stevenson said, 'Don't judge each day by
the harvest you reap but by the seeds you plant.' I first
came across this quote a few years ago while still in my
corporate role. It helped me keep my focus on doing
something each day that took me closer to realising my
dreams. In recognising that I needed to measure my
progress, I acknowledged the only thing I really needed
to measure were the seeds I was planting. The harvest,
after all, is just the outcome of the seeds we plant and
our watering of them – no seeds, no harvest.

It's easy to get disheartened when you feel stuck and
nothing appears to be changing despite all your input,
but you have to trust the process – change is gradual

and sometimes you don't even notice it because the increments are so small.

I remember getting feedback from a friend on how fit and toned I looked. I was over the moon; I'd been consistently going to the gym and exercising four to five times a week for over eighteen months. Because the change in my body shape was so gradual, I didn't notice – I kept going, trusting the process and believing that my enthusiasm would lead me to cultivate the body I wanted. I'm no super model by any stretch of the imagination, but I'm happy that I followed my enthusiasm. I'm fitter now than I was at twenty or thirty.

Don't give up on your dream; it's never too late – take consistent action every single day. You may not reap the harvest until some way down the road, but trust that if you keep planting seeds the harvest will come. Don't worry about the first seed you plant; it might be as simple as taking the time to research what you want for yourself and getting a clearer picture about what you need to fulfil it. Sometimes the only seeds we have to plant are our feelings. Choose to feel good in this moment, choose to feel good today and know that consistently planting these good feelings will ultimately reap a harvest of joy. As a friend once told me, be faithful with the small and the big will come.

What keeps the brakes on?

Knowing yourself is the beginning of all wisdom.
Aristotle

I asked earlier if you were aligned to your hope and the destination you chose for yourself. One of the biggest reasons most people don't take action is not because of fear, but because they aren't actually aligned with where they want to go. Once you know that you are truly aligned to your inner GPS, it's easier to see what else is getting in the way of moving forward.

Many people experience resistance that hinders their attempts to release the handbrake and press on the accelerator. But what do we really understand about resistance? In his book *The War of Art,* Steven Pressfield shares a perspective that really helped me understand the role of resistance – why it shows up and what you need to overcome it.[14]

First, he acknowledges that resistance is universal. Every one of us experiences resistance. Each time you seek to move upwards, to move ahead, to grow, you encounter resistance. Why? Because resistance is a force of nature. Yes, more science. It's helpful to view it as you would gravity: what comes up must come down. Resistance is the opposition to your dreams. The darkness to your

---

14 https://stevenpressfield.com/books/the-war-of-art

light. Where there are dreams, there will always be resistance, the shadows.

Whenever resistance appears, don't judge yourself. If you can realise that when you tell yourself you are not good enough, when the fear kicks in, when the negative voices in your head keep you playing small – it's not you, it's the resistance. While they pretend to be your thoughts, they're not. It's just the negative energy that wants to counteract your evolution. It shows what you don't want so that you can be clearer about what you do want.

The more important something is to you, the greater the resistance. How do you overcome it? Well, there is no silver bullet. It starts with action, the commitment to take action. Steven Pressfield eloquently describes it as 'put your ass where your heart wants to be'.

To go on a journey you must take the first step. You already know where your heart wants to be so don't deny yourself. The first step often comes when the pain of standing still becomes much greater than the pain of moving forward. Sometimes it's when the desire and will for something more are greater than the resistance; you feel impelled to move forward knowing it's where you are meant to go.

If you acknowledge, like gravity, that resistance is always going to be present, then moving past it becomes part of your job. When resistance shows up, you know it's because you are moving closer to your dreams.

The impediment to action, advances action.
What stands in the way becomes the way.
Marcus Aurelius

Resistance appears in many forms: fear, perfectionism, procrastination, limiting beliefs, overwhelm, inertia, hesitation, excuses. Sometimes it looks like you in your PJs not wanting to get out of bed. Resistance wants to beat you into submission in an effort to keep you safe. To keep you in your comfort zone, to spare you any feelings of discomfort.

This is where resistance can become confused with the discomfort of growing. Your growth feels uncomfortable because it's new and it stretches you. Transforming your present is going to be uncomfortable; your discomfort is evidence that you are creating the change you want. Like a caterpillar, before it turns into a beautiful butterfly, it has to navigate the discomfort of changing its form.

I know when I first started exercising, my aching muscles, although painful, were the first indication that I was creating the body I wanted. I didn't need to see immediate results; I knew from my sore muscles that something was changing. It was all the encouragement I needed.

Use your discomfort as an indicator of you planting the seeds for your harvest. Reframe your discomfort as encouragement for what you are creating. And don't forget you are creating something wonderful.

If you want to measure your success, measure your actions. Ask yourself daily – did I overcome any resistance today? And if you did, well done. You are a step closer to realising your dreams.

Consistency compounds

Little by little, one travels far – I have these words framed on the wall in my lounge. They remind me that even the smallest steps consistently move me significantly further forward. I am not standing still. I know it's obvious, but how many of us don't start something we want to do because we believe we don't have the time?

If you were to find just 15 minutes a day over 365 days, you'd have 91 hours. You can get a lot done with 91 focused hours. Stop allowing the resistance to beat you into submission. Start somewhere, start now.

Summary: Move towards your destination

Words don't teach: you have to live something to truly know it. I started this chapter with the acknowledgement that the gap between knowing and doing is huge. Just because the H.E.A.R.T. self-leadership method seems simple, it's not easy – words don't teach, life experience does. You have to put it into practice to really know the feeling of being unstoppable and to create the leadership impact and life you want.

Think of yourself as an onion and start to peel back the layers to find your own truth, however much your eyes might water from being honest with yourself. When it comes to dealing with others, always speak the truth pleasantly; never speak a pleasant untruth – that only keeps you stuck and doing what others often do when they sit in the cheap seats and don't get into the arena. Before you make a move, check that you are facing the right direction. Use your intrinsic motivation to propel yourself forward and turn inertia into momentum for reaching your goals. Remember that only today matters; stay in the present moment. Although resistance will keep appearing on your journey, continue to take steps forward, even if they are small ones. Little by little, one travels far. Your consistency will gradually compound and improve your ability to **A**lways **C**ontinue **T**o **I**gnite **O**utcomes **N**ow.

FIVE

Resilience
Recognise Every Season In Life Is Evolution Not Certain Extinction

Roads were made for journeys, not destinations.
Confucious

Why resilience matters

I never gave much thought to resilience before my divorce. I guess I just figured it was something everyone was born with and not something we actively needed to build. I'd seen my mum's relentless resilience in bringing up my sister and me on her own, but I had never sat down with her and sought to understand how she had cultivated it to keep going. In my corporate life, my experience was that when businesses go through change and challenging times, you just have to knuckle down and work harder. Put in the hours, the necessary work, keep going and do what is expected of you.

According to a report by the Black Dog Institute,[15] today one in five people in Australia suffer from mental illness each year. It's clear that regardless of the amount of resilience we are born with, we need to give greater consideration to cultivating it. I believe we are no longer in a world where we can tell ourselves, 'It's not the knockbacks we experience but how many times we get up that counts,' and then just dust ourselves down and expect to be OK. Increasing suicide rates indicate that we have significantly more to do to keep ourselves well. I never thought I was someone who would experience mental illness, but along with divorce it's another unwanted statistic I have become part of.

When I created the H.E.A.R.T.® self-leadership method, I measured my resilience based on how well I recovered from the break-up of my marriage. I had no idea that tougher years lay ahead and I'd need to go even deeper in building my resilience. That's the problem. It's easy to have a false sense of security thinking that you are resilient without spending any time cultivating it. It's also easy to assume that others have it too: your children, family, friends or your team. You never really think about helping them build their resilience at a deeper level, especially if you haven't considered it yourself.

---

15 www.blackdoginstitute.org.au

In this chapter I reveal a deeper vulnerability than I have up to now. I do this because of my profound belief that we need to shift the immense burden of shame we place on ourselves. The only way I can help do this is by leading the way. I've seen too many people try to lead from behind; ultimately you can't lead that way.

Shifting shame

I share a blog that I wrote on 2 September 2019.

DEPRESSION DOESN'T LOOK LIKE ME DOES IT?

Depression – it's a heavy word and an even heavier feeling. I should know because it's something I've been navigating on and off for the last twenty months.

I remember writing my first blog about it in Jan 2018 with the title 'Find someone to help you paddle'. I described it as the 'funk'. I didn't know why I was feeling so sad and why that feeling had crept up on me, but I recognised that I needed help. Thankfully for me, my family leaned in.

Over the last year since leaving my corporate job and starting my own business, the uncertainty of this new uncharted territory sent my brain into fight, flight or freeze mode. Last Sep to Dec were particularly challenging months with high levels of anxiety and depression. Thankfully, a trip home to England last Christmas connected me again to those who loved me, those who helped me see more clearly when I couldn't for myself. I knew it was bad when I walked into a supermarket and had to walk out because I found it too overwhelming to have to make a decision on what to purchase – my brain was overloaded with stress.

I'm writing this blog today because I wanted to share that I've been fighting the good fight with mental illness. I thought I'd beat it, but I haven't. Not just yet anyway. Last week I found myself in tears a number of times for no apparent reason and felt incredibly sad. There were days where I woke up telling myself a story that I hated my life. This is not true, but it was how I felt – I couldn't shake it off and it frustrated me.

It frustrated me because I've been doing a lot of inner work, leaning into my H.E.A.R.T.° self-leadership method, meditating, being mindful, taking walks in nature, spending quality time with friends, exercising, eating healthier (not quite healthy but healthier), getting the right sleep, drinking water, seeing a psychologist, etc, but I still felt down.

Whilst this may sound silly, I told myself more stories – 'It must be something to do with the moon cycles and the energy pulls affecting my mood' or that 'It's natural I feel stressed because I'm building a business and it's not easy.' Of course, both of these are feasible (yes, the moon can have an impact), but neither were the reason.

The truth is that I've been functioning while being depressed. The ongoing stress of building a business while living on the other side of the world from my family and my oldest friends, living life as an independent empowered woman (without the handsome man, my family or oldest friends around to give me a big hug at the end of each long day and tell me it's going to be OK) are taking their toll.

I've never missed work or spent a day in bed under the covers. I engage with people and work hard, coaching clients and facilitating workshops. Last week I did three live webinar interviews with C-Suite leaders; I laughed and carried myself like a regular 'mentally well' human being. I caught up with friends, had dinners, read books and functioned well. At least that's what it seemed to the outside world, and perhaps to me as well.

But the truth is my depression has been insidious, gradual and sly – giving me the impression it had gone (I never understood why it came in the first place). But in reality, it sits there and appears in my thoughts, hiding under the surface and influencing my outlook of my world. It continues to make me believe that I must be doing something wrong as I am unable to shake off the thoughts that don't serve me.

I've found myself standing at a pedestrian crossing and having a random thought about the bus hitting me. I've spent moments asking myself what's the point and why am I here. I've felt tired even after having a full night's sleep. I've felt there is a grey cloud over my head even when the sky is blue. I smile and laugh but have forgotten the feelings of deep contentment and joy. I find myself forgetting things and then beating myself up because my mind is not as sharp as it once used to be. I've forgotten how to truly relax because I've hardwired a pathway that says I must work harder each day to serve my goal of helping others reveal their power to make change happen.

I'm aware that I need to fill my own cup and only let others drink from the overflow so that I never go empty. It's what I teach my clients but my own brain seems to have other ideas. That's why I know it's not me – because when I know better, I work on doing better.

I sought help this weekend and today I made a decision to take medication to help me strengthen my mind against this insidious illness. Most people don't write about this stuff when they are in it, usually they wait until they've got a success story to share. But when I started this blog, long before I started my business, I vowed I'd always share the lessons I was learning as I was learning them. It's confronting and not easy to speak so openly, but it's necessary.

My business 'Heart of Human' is about empowering wellness, wisdom and wealth; it starts with taking off masks and being real. If I can't do that myself then I can't expect anyone else to do it – I hope in sharing what's going on for me, you'll know it's safe for you to take off your mask too.

I know medication is only part of the journey to re-strengthen my mind and combat this illness, so yesterday (1 Sep) I also joined a beautiful group of women to focus on self-love – posting daily on Instagram to share the journey. Today I danced and laughed and recorded myself being silly – most people on Instagram will see it and think I'm super happy and that my life is wonderful.

My life is wonderful, but it doesn't mean it's easy and that I don't have my challenges – it's actually really hard a lot of the time.

But I'm not giving up on my mission to help others, so I'll lean further and further into my heart – Hope, Energy, Action, Resilience and Trust and start with honouring the need to help myself.

It wasn't easy writing and sharing my story in a blog, but I recognised that in order for us to be truly resilient, we have to shift shame. That can only happen when we take the stigma out of mental illness.

I had to admit that I failed to see how deep I was in my mental illness; I'd lost perspective of myself and my life. I was stuck on a hamster wheel trying to grow a business; I had let everything else go. It was the only thing I ever talked about. Every conversation was about how scared

I was, about not having enough money or how I didn't think I could make it work.

I also had a massive resistance to taking medication and all the stigma attached. I didn't want to add to my feelings of failure by taking meds. It was only when I had suicidal thoughts about the bus hitting me that I really understood that my sadness wasn't normal. Taking anti-depressants actually allowed me to see myself clearly for the first time in a really long time. I started to feel more human again. The fog around me lifted; I didn't feel that dark cloud following me anymore.

I was lucky that I had an incredibly supportive family. My mum and sister were, and continue to be, phenomenal. I also found good friends who I was able to speak to, friends who I didn't feel would judge me. I shared openly with these friends and I was able to move forward with the support I needed.

I had lost other friends earlier that year. One had judged me for my underlying fears and sadness; others weren't able to cope with my anxiety and overwhelm. I don't have any hard feelings towards them. I recognise it can sometimes require you to give a lot of yourself to support others, especially when they are in a dark place. However, I'm sharing this because mental illness cannot be navigated alone. I know that my illness worsened with the sense of isolation I felt when trusted friends weren't able to be there for me.

Today I know that I'm connected to myself in a way that I never previously managed. The journey hasn't been easy, but I recognise that it required me cultivating deep resilience. Essentially that's what I share in this chapter – methods I learned the hard way through my own journey.

Before I describe the steps involved, I want to share another extract from my blog and it is something I've never shared before. I regularly write to myself, for myself, as a way of clearing my head of the narratives it comes up with. I particularly wanted you to see this as it reveals on a deeper level where my thoughts were at that time. I can't remember exactly when I wrote this as I didn't date it, but it was a few months before I got the help I needed. The irony is that because of my high self-awareness of my thoughts and feelings, I believed that I was mentally well – but the reality was the opposite.

Mental illness comes in all shapes and sizes

FEELING TRAPPED IN A PRISON OF MY THOUGHTS

As time passes, I feel an overwhelming fear that I will no longer know what it means to wake up without a sense of dread around me. It's terrible considering I've left a job that wasn't fulfilling and that I spend more time now in a state of unease and confusion about what to do each day.

I wonder whether entrepreneurship is something I can do. I look around and other people appear to have it figured out, but I don't seem to have a clue. I drift in and out of weeks and I wonder whether this passing time will eventually be looked on as making sense or whether it's just a black hole.

It's testing my resolve, but I think for resolve to be effective, you must have absolute clarity on what you seek to deliver as an outcome.

Me speaking out that I want to make a difference doesn't really make me unique, nor does it help with being able to clearly define what I do.

I've spent days and days pondering not only what I should be doing but also how I should be doing it. And as weeks and months pass by, I don't seem to be much closer to the answer.

I've visited the dark depths of depression where I have at times wondered whether there is any point to my existence.

There are moments and sometime days where I see the possibility of a life where I am abundant with happiness and feeling incredibly fulfilled, and then there are those days and weeks and perhaps months that I can't see past the darkness, the confusion in my mind, wondering why I'm here and desperately wishing I had clarity on what I should be doing.

Sometimes I find myself believing that the only way to stop the confusion is for everything to be over. I've never considered actually taking my life, but I've really begun to understand why people do. It's confronting to even acknowledge that it makes sense to me.

How does anyone taking their life make sense? But I can actually empathise – I understand through my own shame. Shame from the times I did ask for help and friends didn't help. Shame for the times I've been embarrassed to admit that I didn't know what to do and instead pretended everything was fine.

Shame when I received a text message from a friend who said she couldn't be friends with me anymore because I shared how overwhelmed I was feeling with her all too often – I had no idea she even felt that I was a burden.

When your psychological safety with people you feel safe with is compromised, then it's pretty confronting.

Truthfully, it's only because of the pain it would cause to my family that I wouldn't go ahead with harming myself. That and perhaps the fear of actually doing it; I've reached lows but thankfully I haven't hit that level.

I have felt like I've been gasping for air inside, drowning in my own negative and all-consuming thoughts. Unable to see progress, unable to see the achievements. All I can see is failure. All I can see is that I'm a failure.

When I read that again, it shows me that mental illness comes in all shapes and sizes. While to the outside world, I was projecting all was good, the insidious nature of mental illness was eating me up on the inside. My coaching clients and the leaders I worked with saw that I was confident and self-assured. I absolutely was for them because I loved working with them; those were the moments I felt most alive. But on the inside, when I was by myself, I felt terrified and anxious for my own survival.

When I look back at this time, I don't recognise myself. How did I let myself get this way? I had failed to understand that resilience needs to be cultivated, especially at a deep level. I failed to understand its importance for my mental wellbeing. In essence, I failed to recognise how misunderstood resilience is.

I developed the 'Resilience Roundabout', ten ways to cultivate resilience. As I take you through them, I show where I failed to apply them so you can see how easy it is to correct. It's helpful for me to share like this as I live and breathe what I describe in this book. I recall Oprah's mantra, 'When you know better, you do better.' This a useful reminder of what I already touched on in the action step: there is a big difference between knowing and doing.

The resilience roundabout

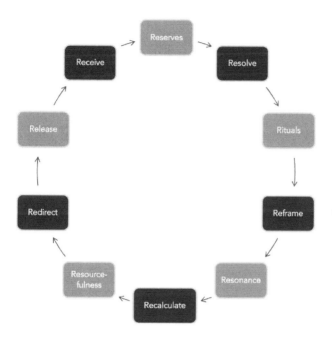

The ten ways to cultivate resilience

1. Reserves
2. Resolve
3. Rituals
4. Reframe
5. Resonance
6. Recalculate
7. Resourcefulness
8. Redirect
9. Release
10. Receive

1. Reserves – how full are your resilience reserves?

When was the last time you considered your resilience reserves in the same way you view your bank balance? Probably never. When it comes to our bank accounts, we know we need to have funds before we can draw any money out. What most of us don't recognise is that the same is true for resilience – you can't draw on reserves you don't have.

While it's pretty easy to see if you have funds in your bank balance, it's less obvious to see if your resilience reserves are full. However, if you consciously ask yourself how full you feel your resilience reserves are, while you might not be able to measure them as accurately as your bank balance, you can probably gauge how full they are. Simply asking the question raises awareness and makes you take stock of your resilience.

When my marriage ended, I knew I had to cultivate resilience. Because my heart was broken, it made sense – I needed resilience to get through. However, when I decided to follow my bliss and leave my corporate role, it didn't occur to me that I would need to cultivate resilience. I felt strong in myself. While I 'knew' the journey would be hard, I didn't truly know. I didn't spend time reflecting on whether my resilience reserves were full enough to support me on the journey.

Had I done so, I would have paid more attention to what I needed, such as a support network of people who had taken the same journey. I should have learned more about what energised me to adjust my environment to support me. Perhaps I should have also acknowledged that my reserves were still at risk having only come out of a 'funk' a few months earlier.

2. Resolve – what is your commitment to yourself?

Resolve is a significant factor in building resilience. Resolve is about the commitment you make to yourself knowing that life being what it is, the going will get tough at times. Think of resolve as a vow you make to yourself; a one-sentence statement that you will hold true to yourself as you navigate life.

Why do you need to make this commitment to yourself?

Nobody wants to fail, even those of us who are prepared to fail for our purpose never want to fail. We just learn how to embrace it and accept it as an inevitable part of our own personal growth. With social media continually showing other people's wonderfully 'successful' lives, there is huge pressure to keep up and curate a life that looks just as good – or better.

Most of us realise that what we see on social media is only half the story at best. The truth is that our greatest growth comes from our most challenging and darkest of times, but it's not something you want to post on Instagram. Nor does anyone really want to choose to experience the darkness just so they can appreciate the light. I've learned through my own journey, however, that we do need this contrast in life to find out who we are and what we want.

I realised that making a commitment to myself, one which acknowledged my resolve, would serve as an anchor when the tough times came. Not having an anchor means it's easy to drift and lose sight of where and sometimes who you are. That's what happened to me; I didn't have a clear resolve and a lack of anchor meant I was drifting.

My resolve is 'I choose to feel good every day and act from inspiration aligned with my heart.'

What is your resolve?

3. Rituals – what keeps you connected to the path, to your destination?

Rituals are about putting your resolve into practice, creating habits that help to honour your commitment to yourself and fill your reserves of resilience. Rituals are repeated either daily, weekly or monthly. They support you by keeping your head clear and your heart aligned so that you keep moving forward along the path you have chosen.

What I realise now was that I had lost the balance in my life; I made work all-consuming. I stopped doing the things that I enjoyed – going for walks, reading fiction, spending regular time with good friends – and I wasn't making time for meditation.

The fear of not having enough money led me to stop socialising. I spent more and more time by myself, living entirely in my own thoughts. Had I maintained healthy rituals that balanced the time I spent working and play-ing, I'd have been in a much better state of mind.

What I see clearly now is that rituals are there to help you keep a consistent rhythm to reach the destination you have set for yourself. They keep you grounded and connected to yourself so that you don't break down on the journey.

4. Reframe – what story do you need to change?

The stories we choose to tell ourselves should be ones that propel us forward.

I was paying no attention to the fact that I was repeating over and over again everything that I was terrified of happening. I chose to tell myself a story of not being good enough; I chose to beat myself up for the leap of faith that I'd made. Instead of acknowledging my courage, I told myself I was an idiot. Instead of seeing the opportunities that lay ahead of me, I looked back at all the things I had given up.

We all have a choice about what we choose to feel and how we view things that happen in our lives. It's easy to think things outside of us – the environment or people – are responsible for our feelings. Reframing perceptions requires consciously considering the world around us and choosing a narrative that serves us, not one that hinders us. We all recognise those around us who are glass-half-full people and always open to finding a way forward. They are better to be around and certainly more resilient because of the way they choose to frame their view of life.

We all have opportunities to reframe. You can consider not getting the job you wanted as a reflection of you not being good enough or as an opportunity for you to learn more about what people are looking for and discern what you really want. You can view someone's feedback as overly critical or try to use it to understand their perception of you and why they have it. You can regard failure as shameful or as an opportunity to collect new data about what doesn't work. We have opportunities to reframe our thinking every single day; it builds our resilience to face even the toughest of challenges.

I continue to learn that we receive what we perceive. If we choose to perceive things as difficult, challenging or impossible, then that's what we receive. If we choose to see opportunity, possibility, ease and flow, then that's what we receive. Our thoughts do become our reality. Changing a story we have on repeat that doesn't contribute to us is one of the most resilience-building steps we can take. More than that, we create the conditions for the life we want to become a reality. If you struggle with this, seek leverage from your support structure.

5. Resonance – how aligned are you with the path you are on?

You might be wondering what resonance has to do with building resilience. It's how you find out if your current destination is still the one you want. I've already mentioned how your purpose can evolve and the destination you choose at the outset may no longer have the same resonance with your heart. It's often easier to keep going down your original path, facing obstacles and getting back up after knockdowns, than question whether your path still has the same resonance for you.

What I learned was that I had no resonance with the way I tried to measure my business in the early days. I had replicated my corporate life by measuring my success based on what I saw as tangible evidence that my new work was of value. The measure I chose for tangible evidence was income. When the income wasn't flowing in those early day, I began to question my own value.

It took me a while to realise that measuring money had absolutely no resonance with me: it wasn't my intrinsic driver. I wanted to do work I loved every day, to have a spring in my step knowing that I was making a difference. I wanted to create something I could be proud to leave as a legacy. I eventually acknowledged that I hadn't left my corporate career for money. After all, I had been earning a good salary in my corporate role while working significantly fewer hours than I was now for myself.

When I transferred my focus and used the measurement of what filled my heart with joy rather than sales revenue, the resonance with my work shifted and I felt so much more fulfilled. I felt happy for the first time in ages; instead of waking up with dread, I looked forward to what would unfold as I followed my joy. This new resonance unblocked my energy and I stopped suffering from anxiety. As a result, opportunities began to come in more regularly with work that aligned perfectly with what I wanted. I felt I was no longer giving off the icky vibes of needing to make a sale – ones I'm sure people could smell a mile off. I allowed myself to have fun and enjoy the conversations about my mission, regardless of whether they might lead to business. If I'd known this earlier, I could have saved myself a lot of pain and mental suffering.

6. Recalculate – what are the alternative pathways?

Just as you get your GPS to recalculate the route when you encounter a roadblock, this step reminds you to reconsider all the available pathways when you first identified your goal. What are the options now? What routes are still open? Sometimes it's necessary to turn around and go back before you find another road that will take you forward again. This doesn't mean you are off-track – consider it recalibration.

When I stepped back to consider what I wanted, I recognised that I didn't have to do things alone. I was letting my ego stop me from engaging support from others, as I felt embarrassed and ashamed to ask for help.

I had spent my entire career in finance with people coming to me because they needed me. Now I felt like a nobody. For the first time, I realised how small and insignificant I was outside my job title and the big brands I worked for. I'd made the all-too-common mistake of attaching my worth to my status, and my ego had taken a hit.

Once I realised this and acknowledged the fact that I was starting at ground zero, I saw that asking others for help wasn't a failing. I was giving others the opportunity to see the value of what I could bring and support me to succeed. I'm glad I got out of my own way and let go of my ego. It allowed me to be supported by people who had been through this journey and could help me achieve the vision I had for my life.

I learned that there are many pathways to the destination we set, but the routes can change depending on where you are in your journey. New paths opened up for me that would never have been available had I not taken the journey to where I was. We can't get life wrong – it always gives us opportunities to recalculate. The decision lies with us to make that choice.

7. Resourcefulness – how are you moving past your limits?

Being resourceful is a wonderful way to build up your resilience. It makes you creative about the options available and helps you to navigate any obstacles. Resourcefulness helps you to see opportunities where others might not and create a way forward by looking at things from different perspectives. Choosing to be resourceful makes problems less about something to fear and more about opportunities to discover new possibilities.

The biggest obstacle I faced when I left my corporate role was learning about sales. I told myself the story that I sucked at it, so I did. Setting sales targets and measuring sales didn't resonate with me at all, but knew that I needed an exchange of fair value for me to keep doing the work I loved and for the impact I planned.

However, I didn't like the idea of being a self-promoter. Until I was comfortable with seeing myself and my value more clearly, the only way I would survive financially was to let others promote my work instead.

I found partners to work with and focused on delivering my best. I knew I would never want to let others down. This approach shifted my view of myself and the value I had to offer. My partners had high standards and shared the same values for what they wanted for their clients. They helped me move my mission forward; I know I certainly wouldn't be where I am without their support. From the positive feedback I received from my clients and my partners, I could see that I had been the obstacle hindering the progress I wanted to see happen, and I realised how much a disservice this was to the women I could help.

I had been stuck in my ego. I had made the story about self-promotion and selling be all about me, about selling myself. The truth is that I was selling a solution to a problem that my clients had. How ironic that I'd fallen into the same trap I was pulling my clients out of. Most of the women I coached hated the idea of self-promotion and didn't want to draw attention to themselves, yet they all wanted to be seen as impactful leaders. Again, it's ironic really, because just like me the work they did wasn't about them, but what they were doing was limiting the positive impact they could have with their teams.

Have you ever stopped yourself from selling your ideas, solutions, problem-solving skills and your leadership? Have you thought that your work speaks for itself and that you don't need to promote it? Is the story you tell yourself that you don't want people to think you are full of yourself?

The truth is we should be full of ourselves – so full that we overflow with what we have to give. I learned through being resourceful that while I had found a short-term solution for my business, I had to solve the root cause of my sales hesitancy – the belief I was selling myself rather than a valuable service. Thankfully, I did that through reframing my story.

8. Redirect – where could you redirect your focus that feels good?

When we feel good anything seems possible. When you've hit obstacle after obstacle and feel deflated, sometimes the only option is to redirect your focus to something that feels good in your life. It may have nothing to do with the path you've set for yourself, but it's important to recognise that what makes us feel good plays a significant role in our resilience.

In my darkest days sleep was what made me feel good. I allowed myself to redirect my attention to switching off and resting. I accepted that while it didn't feel like it was taking me closer to where I wanted to go, it was the respite I needed from thoughts that were making my life a misery. Other times, I chose to go for a run or play music that connected me with happier memories. Sometimes I'd write in my appreciation journal and occasionally I watched funny videos on YouTube as a way of completely switching off from all the things I feared.

Redirecting our thoughts and actions away from ones that don't serve us to ones that do is the fastest way to recovery. The more I focused on redirecting thoughts to what felt good in my life, the less overwhelmed I felt. I began to see possibilities and a much richer and fulfilling life than the scary movie I found myself stuck in.

How often do you replay an old movie in your head that leaves you feeling down? What would you direct your thoughts towards? What would make you feel good?

9. Release – what do you need to let go of?

This step is simple but not easy. It's easy to become attached to the idea of how things should have turned out, but life doesn't work that way. I never imagined being divorced, forty years old, single, no children and recovering from mental illness. It's not exactly my idea of what a dream life looks like. It certainly wasn't the one I chose – at least not consciously.

The contrast between my life today and what I wanted, which was to be happily married with kids, a beautiful dog, growing old happily ever after, is considerable. I learned that if I continued to measure my life from the vantage point of what I didn't have, compared to what I actually did have, it would always fall short. Our desires are always more attractive compared to what we have; as humans that's how we are wired – for getting more. Even when we do have what we want, there is always something else to want. It doesn't mean that we won't be content, just that there's always more out there to want.

I had to let go of my attachment to the life I had wanted and embrace the life I had and seek my joy from travelling on the journey rather than from the arrival at the destination. I also learned to release self-judgement and not to punish myself for occasionally feeling sorry for myself and having moments of sadness. I just allow myself long enough to release the thoughts that are making me unhappy.

Releasing and letting go feels like floating down a gently flowing river. You aren't trying to swim against the current and fight the resistance. It feels peaceful and calm and there is a knowing that you are being carried exactly where you need to be. How often do you feel as though you are swimming upstream? What are you attached to that you need to let go of? What if you could stop swimming, turn onto your back and allow yourself to be carried by the flow – how would that feel?

10. Receive – what can you allow yourself to receive?

People don't generally think that allowing yourself to receive is correlated with building resilience, but it really is. Allowing yourself to receive love and support from others, allowing yourself to receive the wisdom from your own heart, allowing yourself to receive the inspiration and impulses to guide you towards another path and choose a different way, allowing yourself to receive the happiness and abundance for the life you want.

I had to learn how to be honest with myself and how to receive help. I felt some shame at having to receive help from family and friends and also for going on medication for my mental illness. Even though my logical mind was saying that it was for the best, emotionally I wasn't allowing myself to receive the support I needed. I don't know why we punish ourselves this way, but I've realised that allowing myself to receive has made me significantly stronger. It's a core step to building resilience.

I really don't know why we think we should do things on our own, but I'm glad I've learned how to receive love, kindness, compassion and the support I needed to get through my dark days and keep me on track for the destination I set for myself.

One of the main reasons we don't get what we want is the resistance we put in the way. We can say prayers and set intentions, but a lack of belief in ourselves and unwillingness to accept the support of others will always limit what we receive. Allowing ourselves to receive requires us to acknowledge our own worth and see that we deserve everything that we want. Allowing ourselves to receive means surrendering our ego (our conscious mind's sense of self). Often, we don't like to admit that we can't do everything ourselves.

I'm aware that men more than women are more likely to leverage the support of a coach or a mentor. Perhaps it's time for women to acknowledge that we'd be a lot further ahead if we accepted support and guidance – I know that personally I would have progressed further in my career if I'd sought support earlier on.

Although receiving is not what most people associate with building resilience, spend five minutes examining whether you routinely decline offers of help and support. Imagine what impact you could make if you did accept them.

Summary: Recover quickly after setbacks

Resilience is like a roundabout and sometimes we have to go round a few times, but eventually resilience gives us the means to work out which route we need to take. I know how much I underestimated the fact that resilience needs to be cultivated. But now that I have it in my toolkit, I know I will always find my way whenever I get lost. With all the practices I've described I don't get lost so often these days. I am able to keep my resilience reserves up, so I know I'll be fine.

Here is a reminder of the Resilience Roundabout: the ten ways to cultivate your resilience along with the quick questions to ask yourself that will help determine what is needed for you to recover quickly from any setbacks.

Acknowledge that it's inevitable in life to hit obstacles along your path, but it's the speed of your recovery that makes the difference.

1. **Reserves** – how full are your resilience reserves?

2. **Resolve** – what is your commitment to yourself?

3. **Rituals** – what keeps you connected to the path, to your destination?

4. **Reframe** – what story do you need to change?

5. **Resonance** – how aligned are you with the path you are on?

6. **Recalculate** – what are the alternative pathways?

7. **Resourcefulness** – how are you moving past your limits?

8. **Redirect** – where could you redirect your focus that feels good?

9. **Release** – what do you need to let go of?

10. **Receive** – what can you allow yourself to receive?

The world is currently navigating Covid-19. The impact of the pandemic on our financial and emotional wellbeing is significant. If ever there was a test of resilience, it is now. And as I write this, I'm proud to say I genuinely feel optimistic and positive during this period. I feel better than I've ever felt before, and it's because of this I know that my resilience practices are working. Even though the world is topsy-turvy, my inner wellbeing and strength make me feel unstoppable.

In the next chapter we look at trust – something that is needed more than ever during this time of uncertainty.

SIX

TRUST
Truth Reveals Universal Strength Today

Your heart knows the way. Run in that direction.
Rumi

When it comes to being unstoppable, trust is fundamental to revealing who we truly are and allowing ourselves to discover the potential within. It has become clear to me that if we don't have trust in ourselves, others and the universe, it's impossible to unlock the unlimited possibilities available to us.

Most of what I've learned about trust can't be explained by the logical and rational perspectives of the physical world. Trust isn't something tangible, but we all recognise when it's present and notice when it's absent. I've also learned that trust requires consistently choosing to let go, and as I described in the release section in the last chapter, allowing yourself to be guided so that you can receive the direction and clarity of your path.

In the words of Eckhart Tolle, 'Sometimes surrender means giving up trying to understand, and becoming comfortable with not knowing.'[16] This deliberate surrender to trust was new to me, but it was something I discovered was necessary after I removed a significant amount of certainty from my life. I understand now that the further I travel along this path called life, the more I discover how little I actually know. Despite the continued level of uncertainty that I face, by allowing myself to have trust and faith I've cultivated an inner confidence for the life I've chosen. I'm aware that this allowing of trust will continue to be a lifetime of opting to relinquish control, but by choosing trust on a daily basis, I know that I have access to a world that wouldn't otherwise be available to me. It is a world that I didn't even know existed because previously I chose to live in an environment of measurable certainty.

When I first thought about writing this book in 2017, I thought this chapter on trust would be about how I trusted that my relocation to Australia was going to happen and it did; how I'd learned about trusting in life from my mum's journey and the many challenges she faced but always came out smiling. I didn't know that by the time of writing, my biggest lesson in trust would come from experiencing mental illness. So it's about how I used

---

16 E Tolle, *Stillness Speaks* (Yellow Kite, 2016), p72

trust to cultivate my inner confidence to guide me out of depression and become the unstoppable leader of my life. I'll be candid with you; it's the step in the H.E.A.R.T.® self-leadership method that I found the most challenging. It still is sometimes. I honestly don't think I really knew what trust was until this experience.

Growing up in a single-parent household meant I took responsibility for myself at a young age. We didn't have much money growing up. When I was fifteen, I started working weekends so that I could earn money of my own and relieve some of the pressure on my mum to give me pocket money. I had part-time jobs throughout my university years; I worked four days a week, juggling my study schedule around my job. I didn't take a gap year to travel and I focused on creating a secure life for myself. I bought my first apartment within six months of graduating. I had left university without any debt as I had paid my own way. There were no university grants at the time and I am grateful that university fees only started in my final year, as it would probably be a different story today.

I worked hard and created a safe and comfortable life for myself. I could holiday abroad several times a year, I drove a nice car, and other than my mortgage I had no debts. I was a qualified management accountant in a safe job. I'd never been made redundant; I'd never not had a job since the age of fifteen and I had an income that increased annually with a salary that landed in my bank account each month. This context might help you understand that when I left my corporate job at the age of thirty-eight, it was the first time I faced not having a steady income.

I also didn't leave my secure job in a way I now advise to most people. I didn't build up an income stream in a side business before leaving. I didn't progressively grow the business and reduce my reliance on my corporate salary, steadily cutting down my hours as I generated this income stream. Instead I made one huge leap and left my corporate career with only one coaching client signed up and a truckload of enthusiasm and belief in myself. However, my self-confidence began to wane along with my bank balance; months were going by with minimal income. While I had calculated the numbers and had adequate funds to cover my living expenses for up to two years, fear began to build up inside me as I watched my savings diminish. The uncertainty I was navigating caused my brain to imagine the worst-case scenarios – homelessness and losing everything I'd worked so hard for all my life. I chastised myself for being so naïve.

I had worked in finance for global companies and under-stood business intimately. However, there were some big differences: I'd never started a business from scratch; I was living in a country that was relatively new to me; I had no personal brand to speak of and I was attempting to run a business in a completely new field to the one I'd spent my entire career in. As I keep mentioning, there is a huge gap between knowing about something and actually doing it. My experience of the reality of business showed me how much I didn't know that I didn't know.

I now see how the odds were stacked against me; I'm not surprised that I found myself facing depression and anxiety given the safe and certain world I had embraced for so long. But the biggest revelation about why I found myself in depression was that I had become disconnected to myself. I felt powerless to change the situation I found myself in. I had a loss of faith: essentially, I lost trust in myself.

It sounds silly because everyone I spoke to would say, 'You can always get a job back in finance if things don't work out.' In truth I could, but my brain had already ruled out that option for me. I knew the leap I took was so big that going back wasn't a choice I was making available for myself. I can now also see that without leveraging trust I increased the pressure to succeed in a way that was detrimental to both my physical and mental health. I hadn't realised then how important the role of trust is in succeeding at life. I had only known trust on a surface level; I hadn't appreciated its power to cultivate inner confidence and build the necessary strength to feel unstoppable.

Finding trust again

To survive I had to find trust in myself again. I needed the confidence that everything was going to be OK, even though I couldn't see it then. I've learned a whole heap about trust and the different ways in which we build our trust. Whether it's trust in ourselves, in others or trust in a greater power. I recall a story that my mum told me about her journey in trust. It wasn't long after my dad had left us, and she was navigating how to put food on the table with no financial support. She described a time when she was so hungry and craved a banana, but had no money to buy one.

She was going to the local Gurdwara (Sikh temple) for food; the community kitchen offered free meals to all visitors. On the way, she was having a conversation with God, acknowledging that if only she had some money she would buy a banana to satisfy her craving. Just then she found a one-pound coin on the pavement and was both surprised and shocked that her prayers were not only heard but answered. In that moment she made a decision to trust fully in God's ability to help her when she needed it the most. Her faith has been unwavering ever since. She is one of the happiest and content people I know – she's still unstoppable.

I had some belief in God when I was growing up, but it wasn't my thing. I had perhaps confused the idea that you had to be religious to believe in God. I'd always rebelled against religion from a young age. I didn't like the idea of being told what to do and what others deemed to be right or wrong, or the sense of judgement that I felt religion often imposed. I'd always had an innate belief that humans should feel free to be themselves and express who they are. I acknowledge that religion has its place and I'm not diminishing its value, but personally I chose not to subscribe. What I learned through experiencing my depression is that while I wasn't religious, I did recognise a strong need to believe in something, especially since I didn't believe in myself.

Depression gave me a huge sense of powerlessness, so I was looking for empowerment. I recognised I needed to lean on a belief in something outside myself to support me. Otherwise, I couldn't see how to find my way out of the darkness surrounding me. I needed trust in something to see the light. I was in a state of despair and I know this absence of trust made me feel I was facing a black hole with no escape. I'd already found out through this dark period that I couldn't always depend on people being there for me. Even if they wanted to, it wasn't realistic or reasonable to expect it. As disappointing as this was, I realised then that no-one was specifically put on this earth to make me feel loved, safe and secure throughout my entire life. I had to learn how to do this for myself and it started with understanding trust.

What is trust?

A dictionary definition describes trust as 'a firm belief in the reliability, truth, ability, or strength of someone or something'.[17] Personally, I don't feel this goes far enough

---

17   www.lexico.com/en/definition/trust

in explaining the depth and meaning of what having trust involves. Trust in its fullest expression is an unshakeable belief. Some might go further and acknowledge it as faith. It is a deep level of confidence, whether it be in yourself, in others, the universe, god, source, spirit (pick the one that suits you best) or something else entirely. Trust is believing that when you leap, a net appears. Trust is a sense of knowing that even though you can't see it, you will be guided safely with the belief that any experiences you have along the way serve a greater purpose.

Trust holds us together and, in Stephen Covey's words, 'Trust is the glue of life.'

Where does trust come from?

Trust is something we are all born with but which we often lose in our efforts to create certainty in our lives. As babies, we had trust that when we cried someone would come and tend to our needs. As toddlers, when we learned to speak we were more than comfortable say- ing 'no' without ever doubting that we would be loved any less. As children, we dreamed big without limits and trusted in our own greatness without judging ourselves or our abilities. Somewhere along the way we lose that inner confidence, the trust in ourselves. We begin to doubt ourselves and question our greatness. It is where the journey to find our way back begins. The journey to rediscover the truth of our universal strength.

Nature gives us many clues about what it means to trust and also shows us the connection we have to something greater than ourselves. If you acknowledge trust in the context of creation, when you were growing in your mother's womb your body knew exactly what to do. You didn't have to try and control the timeline of your birth; things unfolded without your input. As a child with grazed knees you trusted in your body's ability to heal your wounds; you didn't question how it happened, you just trusted that it would. As an adult, you go to bed each evening with the trust that you will wake in the morning. Without questioning it, you trust your heart to continue beating and circulate oxygen around your body.

An innate level of trust exists in each one of us and in our connection to the world around us. You can see many examples where our trust is in play, usually evidenced in the natural flow of life where there is no conscious seeking of certainty, just an allowing of what is and what will be.

What happens in the absence of trust?

In the absence of trust, you experience doubt and lack of belief. In the absence of trust, you seek certainty. Certainty sounds great on the surface; we all want to know that everything is going to be OK in our lives. The truth is that the greatest adventure in life comes from its uncertainty. Imagine if your life was like a package holiday – you know exactly where you are going each day, what activities you are doing, where you are staying and who you are with for the entire trip. It doesn't sound that appealing to have this level of certainty for an entire lifetime. We often seek to create certainty in an effort to compensate for the fear in our lives, but by doing so we limit all that is available to us if we allow ourselves to trust. With certainty comes the illusion of having control over our lives; the absence of this illusion induces fear. When fear stalks us, it's difficult to shake it off, and in our efforts to free ourselves from its grip, our resistance to fear only increases its hold.

If you welcome fear without resistance, it actually loosens its hold and its power diminishes. As you read this you may be shaking your head, 'Welcoming fear? Yeah right.' But it is true. Seeking certainty and control in the absence of trust only increases the level of fear that exists in your life. Trust allows us to embrace our fears in the knowledge that we are being supported and held – even though we can't see this certainty, we feel it.

What does trust do for you?

Having trust allows you to open up to the wonder of the world you live in. It puts at your service the universal laws of attraction. Trust feeds your hope for a better future; you see more of what is possible and you open yourself up to these opportunities. Trust gives you a psychological safety net; when you have trust you are more likely to experiment and try new things. When you feel safe you are much braver; there is less fear and less resistance. Trust also allows you to experience love more deeply; it enables you to speak your truth without fear of rejection. Trust gives you the capacity to lean on others without fearing any rebuke; it deepens your connections with others and helps you create a life with greater depth and meaning. Have you ever noticed how your energy is different when you trust? Have you noticed how much calmer and lighter you feel? Have you noticed how you begin to attract when trusting that everything is working out for you?

When we lose belief in ourselves or in our hope for a better future, trust can restore our hopes and beliefs. With trust we can enrol others on a journey and inspire action for a better, more connected world. It makes us more generous in our giving too. When we have trust that everything is working out for us then we are better equipped to help others reach that truth too. We love deeper because trust requires us to connect to a source greater than ourselves. Therefore, we don't fear rejection in the same way we do when trust is absent. Trust allows us to be more present in the moment because it gives us freedom from worrying about the future or dwelling on regrets from the past. The power that trust carries is immense. Allowing yourself to believe in something you cannot see creates endless possibilities of discovering new things and unlocking your fullest potential.

How do you lose trust?

At times of increased uncertainty, as I found, it's not uncommon to start questioning your trust. Especially when unexpected things happen or when they don't happen according to the timeline you set for yourself. Your own expectations, along with the expectation of others, about what your life should look like and how you should be experiencing it, also impact your trust levels. Trust requires surrendering to what is, which is easy when things are going well, but much more difficult when they aren't.

I lost trust from continuing to focus on how my life looked as opposed to the life I desired to create. When I left England in 2015, I had sadness for what I was leaving behind but also excitement for my new chapter ahead. At the time I had trust that I was going to move on and not mourn the past for too long. Trust that I would embrace and create a wonderful new life in Sydney. I lost trust when years later the loving committed relationship I was seeking still hadn't materialised, that I didn't have the children I dreamed of having, that my friendships were still evolving and I wasn't feeling as settled as I had hoped. I'd also left the comfort of my corporate career to follow my bliss, only to find that the reality I created for myself was far from blissful. My life didn't look anything like I expected it to at this point, and by continuing to dwell on the reality I was experiencing and looking at my future through this lens, I was losing hope for my desires and losing trust in my ability to ever realise them.

This is when trusting can be hard, especially when you can't see why things aren't the way you envisaged them to be. It can be hard to stay with trust and keep telling yourself that everything that has unfolded so far has been good for your growth and for the best. I certainly didn't feel like that at the time, but I can see the truth in it now.

Trust vs certainty

It's worth knowing that trust can only exist in the absence of certainty. If there is certainty, there's no need for trust. Many people don't realise this and will always seek certainty. This stops them from leveraging trust to play a bigger game. Certainty, I've discovered, keeps you playing small and limiting your potential to bring about the life you want.

If you are familiar with Maslow's Hierarchy of Needs, two characteristics of self-actualised people are that they welcome the unknown and they are detached from the outcome. Many of us find it difficult to trust because we are so attached to the outcome. We struggle with ambiguity and uncertainty and therefore never seek to lean on trust. Instead we look for areas in our life where we can be certain. I understand now why so many people tell me I'm brave for leaving my corporate career. It's because they can't imagine dealing with the uncertainty of not having a regular income and coping with the ambiguity of the new landscape they'd have to navigate. Trust enables us to take risks; it's not about being reckless, but understanding that a deep level of trust allows us to access a sense of knowing and a belief that gives us the strength to move forward with confidence.

The definition of trust from Brené Brown, which is particularly applicable to building trusting relationships with others, is helpful in adding further context to what it means to trust. She defines trust as 'choosing to make something important to you vulnerable to the actions of someone else.'

This is a powerful insight – most of us dread the thought of being vulnerable and exposed. To be vulnerable and to trust is to be detached from the expectations we have about how others perceive us. It also means we have to be willing to be seen. I've learned that if I want people to be trusting of me then I must extend trust to them, even when I'm in the darkness, even when I'm falling. That's what it looks like to be truly vulnerable in trust.

How do you find trust?

This is a question I had to ask myself again and again when I had lost trust in both myself and the world around me. When I was lost, trust is what I needed to find myself again. It's easy to lose trust when you can't see what you want in front of you. Learning how to cultivate trust is only possible when you don't have certainty about what the future holds for you. It took me knowing what the absence of trust felt like, and the black hole I faced in my depression, to realise that I needed to have a deeper level of trust to uncover the wonder that life had in store for me. In experiencing a loss of faith in myself, others and the environment around me, I had to dig deep. I remembered that appreciation and gratitude go a long way in showing me how much I have to be thankful for in my life. Things I still appreciate today, such as the beauty of Sydney, a city that never fails to put a smile on my face, and more importantly, my health and wellbeing.

Appreciation and gratitude were only part of my journey. I had to find trust in something that I believed would never leave my side; something that would always be available to me. I found trust in god/universe/source/spirit – I don't have a definitive name and I use them interchangeably. It doesn't matter which I use, because the essence is the same – I choose to believe deeply in something I cannot see. Today I have deep faith that I am being held, supported and loved. As a result I've been able to see myself more clearly and cultivate the inner confidence that I know is my true nature.

It is difficult to trust something we can't see. As humans, we like doing things and we thrive on the sense of accomplishment when we make these things happen. Trust isn't about making things happen; it's about surrendering to allow things to happen. This is the opposite of what we've been taught, and contrary to what most people naturally feel inclined to do, especially when they experience uncertainty and feel out of control.

Giving up trust to the universe has been scary. However, I believe that my mental health suffered because I expected to navigate uncertainty by myself. I didn't leverage the trust in a power greater than myself; I didn't surrender myself to a power I could not see. As a result, I didn't allow for the opportunity to be guided or for things to simply unfold. I tried to make things happen, and as a result of pushing myself I was replaying my fears constantly in my mind. I sought certainty where none was to be found.

The importance of the sense of trust

Sometimes you can't believe what you see,
you have to believe what you feel.[18]
Morrie Schwartz

I remember a friend once telling me, 'What's meant for you won't pass you.' I'm now anchored to that belief. By choosing to think about life this way, it connects me to trust. When I left my corporate career, I took a leap without knowing if the net was there to catch me. Starting a new business was and is the biggest risk I've taken in my life. Every day it requires

---

18   M Albom, *Tuesday's With Morrie* (Sphere, 2017)

me to lean into my trust as there is no certainty of success. We often strive hard to get the things we want and keep pushing and pushing to move forward. I find it easier to allow something to happen, and have trust and faith that it will, than endure the struggle to hold onto certainty and control. I learned through belief in a greater power that this was my route back to trusting myself and cultivating an inner confidence to feel unstoppable.

While I had chosen to trust in a power greater than myself, the only way I knew I was really trusting this power was by paying attention to what I was feeling. It can be difficult to acknowledge trust in something you cannot see, but it's much easier to know trust through what you feel.

I mentioned in the power of heart chapter that we all have a source of valuable intuition that is available through our hearts. It is a sense of knowing that comes to us in a sudden thought or flash of insight. It is the 'aha' moment when the dots connect and everything falls into place. Through trusting in a power greater than myself, I was able to allow my heart access to this intuition.

By being aware of how we feel, we allow ourselves to access this powerful guidance that is available to us from our hearts. When we feel good there is coherence between heart and mind; we are better connected to ourselves and it is easier to access these moments of clarity and 'aha'. Feeling good also helps us have the courage to follow the guidance we receive; we can see clearly how the dots connect. When we feel fear our primary guiding force is our body trying to keep us safe. When we are fearful and anxious all our attention is on survival; there is no clarity or space to receive intuition.

Being aware of your feelings and reaching for what feels good allow the guidance and intuition to be clearly received. When you choose to feel good you choose to go with your natural flow. When you feel good you demonstrate being at peace with your present; it means you drop any resistance to not yet having your desired future and enables you to get there faster. It was through choosing to feel good every day that I began to see how I was nurturing trust in myself to leverage the power of the universe. At first, I was terrified of surrendering; I hadn't realised how much I was trying to control my life and how much I was trying to protect myself with certainty. By actively choosing to feel good I had to let go of the activities that gave me a sense of control, but were also imprisoning me in my depression. I had to stop working every single day; I had to choose to take time off to relax, even though I still hadn't created the financial security I craved. I felt immense discomfort at doing nothing, but physically, emotionally and mentally I benefited from taking a break. I had to walk away from the activities such as business development that left me drained. Although it was critical to growing my business, I had to trust that the energy I brought to it wasn't aligned; it was better to stop.

I started meditating and it helped clear my mind. Gradually I began to allow myself to spend money doing things that brought me joy, even though it meant I was spending more than I was earning. I also started making time to catch up with friends more regularly. While I felt guilty for not being at my computer, I recognised that I had been cutting myself off from a support structure that could help me recover from depression. I made these choices to feel good, but they required me to trust that I would be supported. While my brain was afraid, I continued to observe my feelings closely and let them be my guide.

Before long, I began to sense a shift in my perspective; by choosing to feel good I was allowing more possibilities into my life. I started to believe that everything was going to work out. Even though there was no change in my actual circumstances, it was interesting to observe that my energy levels had increased. I also noticed that by choosing to feel good and meditating I managed to reduce the negative chatter of my inner voice. It was becoming quieter and quieter each day.

As the negative chatter began to fade, I started seeing myself more clearly, which led to a significant breakthrough in my ability to trust. I realised that I had been making up trust-limiting stories all my life to protect myself and keep me safe and secure. The only way to know real trust was to let go of these trust-limiting stories. I was petrified at the thought. The biggest trust-limiting story I had to let go of was the one I had created when my dad left. As a child we trust that our parents will always be there for us. When my dad abandoned us, my three-year-old self unconsciously interpreted this to mean that she was unlovable and that people she cared about would abandon her.

I hadn't realised that this three-year-old girl created this trust-limiting story to keep her safe. This story had been playing out all my life and yet I had no idea. I had spent my entire life seeking certainty and searching for evidence of this truth. In every relationship, whether friendships, romantic relationships, professional relationships and latterly client relationships, I expected people either to abandon me or to not choose me in the first place. By creating this story, I had been actively rejecting myself since the age of three, just to have that sense of certainty in my life so that I could feel in control.

It was eye-opening to find this out. I could see how by seeking certainty and security in my life I had cut myself off from trusting others. I had also cut myself off from being my true self. I realised that the depression I had experienced wasn't solely from leaving my corporate career and throwing myself in at the deep end. I realised I had eroded my self-confidence through the unconscious rejection of myself over all these years.

By choosing to feel good I allowed myself to slowly feel my way back to trust and be open to receiving wisdom and guidance from my heart and a power greater than myself. I had no idea that this was what I was going to discover in my journey of trusting myself. After connecting the dots and realising this, I knew that if I was ever to know deep trust, I had to let this story go. It wasn't serving me, and it was keeping me playing small by stopping me from knowing my own true magnificence. In allowing myself to be open to deep trust, I now had faith that I would always be held and supported by a power greater than myself. I finally recognised that I didn't have to fear rejection anymore because I had accessed a level of trust and love from the universe that was deep in my heart. A level that meant I would never feel as though I was journeying alone in life regardless of what was happening in the world around me.

My journey of deep trust started with choosing to feeling good. It was supported by acknowledging that I had complete trust in my mum and my sister and in their love and prayers to keep me safe. I also had trust in longstanding friendships; I knew that these friends had faith in me when I didn't have faith in myself. I allowed myself to trust that the universe was there to listen whenever I needed to speak. Finally, by observing my feelings, I was guided back to my truth and to my connection with my heart, the source of the true intuitive power of the universe.

In acknowledging all my fears and confronting the trust-limiting stories I had created, I enabled myself to discover that Truth Reveals Universal Strength Today – that is what trust is all about. I couldn't feel stronger and more unstoppable than I do now.

Summary: Cultivate your confidence

The journey of trust is all about cultivating confidence and, as I found in my own journey, trust is the hardest step in the self leadership method. The level of trust and confidence you seek is available to you. Here is a summary of how to access it. Consider trust as the **LIGHT** illuminating your path as you move towards your dreams:

The Trust LIGHT

Let Go – surrender your need for knowing and having certainty and control. Let go of your expectations of what you think your life is supposed to look like to allow for it to unfold.

Insight – search inside yourself and explore your own connection to a source of trust. What do you believe in that you cannot see? Look for insight in any trust-limiting stories you may have – where have you been seeking certainty in your life?

Give – to yourself and others from an intention of love and kindness, and generously assume positive intent. We all are human, and we will falter. Building trust requires us to give to ourselves and others without judgement.

Hope – remember your vision of a better future and have faith that the pathway to it will appear. There is a virtuous circle between hope and trust – when we share our hopes with others, we can enrol them on our journeys.

Truth – seek the truth and speak the truth and you will find your way to trust. We all know the inner feeling we get when we aren't honest with ourselves and others; it erodes trust. As I've learned through the School of Practical Philosophy, 'Speak the truth pleasantly and never speak a pleasant untruth.'[19] Truth reveals your universal strength today.

It's time, Unstoppable Woman, to gently let go and know that you are always held and supported. You have travelled with me this far and learned about my journey, now it's your time to focus ahead to the journey you are embarking on to become an Unstoppable Woman.

19 https://practicalphilosophy.org.au

SEVEN

'You Always Had The Power, My Dear'

Now that you've read about my journey to my H.E.A.R.T.® and hopefully had time to reflect on your own journey, I want to bring the concepts I've shared in this book together using one of my favourite children's stories to illustrate how powerful we are when we begin to see ourselves clearly.

The Wizard of Oz – a metaphor for life

In *The Wizard of Oz*, Dorothy travels down the yellow brick road to find the Wizard, in the hope that he can help her get back home to Kansas after she was uprooted by a tornado. When she eventually arrives at Oz and discovers the Wizard is nothing more than a regular human and unlikely to get her home, Dorothy is reminded by the

Good Witch Glinda that she already has the power to get home and that she just has to learn it for herself. The metaphor from *The Wizard of Oz* is the metaphor of our life and also the premise of this book. We have always had the power within us to be unstoppable, but we each need to learn this for ourselves.

If the Good Witch Glinda had told Dorothy at the beginning of her journey that she always had the power to get back to Kansas, Dorothy wouldn't have believed her. She had to undertake the journey to learn it for herself. I acknowledge that if someone had told me I had to reveal the power of my heart to discover how to be unstoppable in my life, I wouldn't have believed it either. Having gone through my own journey down the yellow brick road, seeking my own Wizard to help me find my way home, I discovered the same truth that Dorothy did, that I always had the power within me to find my way home.

My journey will of course be different to yours, but the path we travel is the same. We have to stop thinking that other people have superpowers that we don't have. We have to allow ourselves to dream and to tune into what our hearts know are the lives we desire. We have to care more about feeling good every day and choosing a life that supports this feeling, than we do caring about what other people think.

Remember how the Scarecrow was seeking a brain? And that he too had to learn for himself that he had wisdom all along? I remember that he was given a Diploma Certificate by the Wizard, which, ultimately, we all know did nothing to change who he was or his abilities. This reminds me of the validation we seek from others to say we are good enough. The truth is that others telling us that we are good enough doesn't change us on the inside; we already are good enough. The HeartMath Institute's work on heart and mind coherence shows that the heart sends more signals to the brain than the other way around.[20] Connecting to your heart and allowing the wisdom of your inner self to shine will always lead you to living a richer and more fulfilling life.

The Lion, you may remember, was seeking courage because he was so scared, but he too had to learn for himself that he was already brave. Sometimes we find ourselves fearing what others think about us, but we must remember that courage comes from within. The word courage is derived from Latin word 'cor' which means heart. We all have to find the courage to speak our truth and live our truth. Not only is courage found in our hearts, it is found at the centre of H.E.A.R.T., in action. Courage is action: to act in spite of your fears is the key to courage.

The last character, the Tin Man, was seeking a heart from the Wizard, yet he is already the kindest, most compassionate and emotionally intelligent of all Dorothy's companions. We often fail to extend our loving hearts to

---

20 www.heartmath.org/science

ourselves. Through acknowledging our own hearts and showing ourselves the kindness and compassion that we show others, we can better serve those around us. By tending to our own needs for compassion, we can give to others from a place of abundance rather than depletion.

Each of us knows how precious life is, yet we live as though we are never going to die. Many of us only start truly living when confronted with mortality – it doesn't need to be this way. However, it does require consciously choosing and living the life that you would be most enthusiastic about every single day.

Each and every one of us has the power of our hearts to be unstoppable. All we've ever needed to learn is how to tune into the right frequency of our hearts to leverage this power. You have to choose the station you want to listen to. If what you're listening to doesn't make you feel good, then change the station.

As we discover our own unstoppable power, then it's up to us to enrol others on the journey to find their hearts and their power too. Collectively, through knowing our magnificent unstoppable selves, we can help others access their magnificence too.

EIGHT

Hello Unstoppable Woman

Did you reveal the power of your H.E.A.R.T.®?

While this book shares my journey, it isn't about me. I've written it with the intention of helping you discover the power of your heart, to know who you are and find your own freedom from the enemy within.

The H.E.A.R.T. self-leadership method is incredibly power-ful for the leadership of your life. Now is the time to create the leadership impact and live the life you really want.

Step 1: HOPE
How Our Purpose Evolves

Your purpose will continually evolve; please don't judge your life for the non-linear path it presents you. You have the wisdom to discern your north star. Ultimately, only you know how you want to measure your life; please don't forget that.

Acknowledge hope as your inner **GPS** guiding you towards what your heart really wants. Set yourself the **G**oals that move you towards your north star, explore the different **P**athways, of which there are always many, and instil your **S**elf-Belief. Remember what Abraham Hicks said, 'Your belief is just the thoughts you keep thinking.' Please choose thoughts that help you reach your dreams.

You'll know you are on the right path when you have heart and mind coherence; you feel it when both and heart and mind are aligned. You may feel apprehension and excitement for embarking on the journey, but there will be no doubt in your body about the path you should take.

Step 2: ENERGY
Enthusiasm **N**ot **E**ffort
Resourcefully **G**rows **Y**ou

Your big dreams mean that you need a sustainable source of energy to fill your tank to reach them. Remember to always choose enthusiasm over effort. Fuel yourself mentally, physically, emotionally and spiritually. Don't get distracted and start filling someone else's tank – make sure yours is full before you distribute any surplus fuel.

Remember to notice what fuels you and what drains you – clues to what you need to reach the destination. You don't need an empty tank for starters.

Don't forget the role comparison plays in guiding you to your joy and reconnecting you to what your inner self knows about what you want and what you are capable of being and doing.

Step 3: ACTION
Always Continue To Ignite Outcomes Now

The present moment matters. Focus on planting the right seeds and you'll get to reap the harvest you seek. There are many wake-up calls in life that ask us to look a little bit closer and deeper at the life we are living, and the person we are choosing to be. It's never too late to start creating the life and leadership you want. Don't forget that courage is action and that to know something you have to be or do something. You know it's time to release the handbrake and accelerate towards the life you want. Check you are facing in the right direction and let your inspiration turn inertia into momentum for change. Be prepared for resistance, but know that each small, consistent step you take compounds and you will soon see that you will reach your destination.

Step 4: RESILIENCE
Recognise Every Season In Life Is
Evolution Not Certain Extinction

One thing I know about life is that it always involves setbacks and obstacles. This is an inevitable truth. My biggest growth came through adversity; it's likely yours will too. Let's not pretend you won't face any challenges. It's time to shift any shame you have around failing and leverage your resilience to keep on moving. Successful leaders cultivate resilience so they have reserves when they need them – use the resilience roundabout to help you understand what would help you recover quickly and go forward stronger. Focus on the big picture of your life and acknowledge there will always be changing seasons.

Step 5: TRUST
Truth Reveals Universal Strength Today

Trust is a significant foundation in revealing who we truly are and allowing ourselves to see the potential within us and others. Remember our trust light to move forward, even when we can't see the road ahead. Embrace the uncertainty. Choose to trust in what you cannot see and choose to consistently feel good. Our future is not created by looking at our current reality but through the desires, visions and aspirations we hope to fulfil. Allow yourself to trust that everything you need is already within you – there will be times of doubt but remember, trust is only present in the absence of certainty. Your truth will reveal your universal strength; let go of your trust-limiting stories and access the power of your heart to provide the wisdom that will guide your path.

Why does it matter?

The promise of this book is to reveal the power of your heart to create leadership impact and cultivate confidence for the life you want.

When most people think of leadership, it's usually leadership in business. This book isn't a traditional business leadership book, but I know that when you do life leadership well, in particular self-leadership, you are exponentially more effective as a leader in business and in leading others.

In writing this book my intention is to help you access your inner truth and reconnect to your heart so that you can begin to see for yourself how unstoppable you are. As a female leader, by revealing the power of your H.E.A.R.T. you can have an equal seat at any table, whether it's the board table or a kitchen table. My desire is for you to have choice and an equal seat wherever you decide to sit.

This book required me to go deep in sharing my own journey and face the reality of the path I've been on – for which I thank you. I couldn't know for sure until I started writing this book that I would be able to get the words out and share my story as I have. Having you in mind gave me the momentum to keep going, taking little steps every single day to meet you and show up for you. I believe in you and I believe between us we can create the change we want to see in this world.

I don't want us to play small; we have work to do. If we are to change the landscape of business from one of patriarchy and alpha male leadership as the dominant role model, we need to own the power of female and recognise strength in balance.

I want the world to look different. I want there be gender equality. It starts with us seeing ourselves clearly and recognising that leading with H.E.A.R.T. isn't a weakness but a huge strength.

One of my favourite quotes is from Margaret J Wheatley – 'There is no power for change greater than a community discovering what it cares about.'[21] By reading this book I hope you choose to be part of this community of unstoppable women who are revealing the power of their hearts to make change happen.

Be an Unstoppable Woman. Be You.

---

21 MJ Wheatley, *Turning to One Another* (Berrett-Koehler Publishers, 2002), https://margaretwheatley.com

Next steps

To access further resources to support you in becoming an Unstoppable Woman, visit my website: www.heartofhuman.com

Unstoppable Human Scorecard

Knowing where to start can be the hardest step; try measuring what's getting in your way.

The Unstoppable Human Scorecard is designed to measure your current self-leadership based on the H.E.A.R.T.® self-leadership method. You receive an overall score for the power of your heart and a score for each step of the method, along with guidance on how to improve each aspect of your self-leadership to create the leadership impact you desire and live a life you love.

Visit www.heartofhuman.com and click on the link on the home page to access.

Discover your unstoppable power

This is a self-reflection workbook with key questions for you to answer that will help you discover your unstoppable power. As you already have what you need within you, this is an opportunity to draw it out so that you can see things clearly for yourself on where to focus next.

Visit www.heartofhuman.com and click on the link on the home page to access.

Join the community and learn more about being an Unstoppable Woman

in www.linkedin.com/company/heartofhuman

f @heartofhumanofficial

⃝ @heartofhumanofficial

Acknowledgements

To all the heart-centred humans that have helped me bring this book to life, my deepest appreciation. Taking this step has been much easier with your support, guidance and encouragement.

Thank you to the wonderful team at Rethink Press who have kept me honest with the timelines for getting this book completed and published, for guiding me gently through the entire process and for helping me craft my message in a way that I could never have accomplished on my own. A special thanks to Eve Makepeace for project managing with such grace, commitment and focus to helping me publish a book that I'm proud to share.

A huge thank you to my beautiful mum and gorgeous sister Rosie for the ongoing encouragement and for supporting me in sharing a personal and vulnerable family journey so that others can see what is possible when your purpose is bigger than your fears.

Thank you to my oldest best girlfriends Kat, Kate, Helen, Emilia, Suzy, Lisa and Rav for continuing to love and support me even though I live on the other side of the world and rarely get to see you. We may not see each other often but we always pick up where we left off; that's the sign of true lasting friendship. Your belief in me has never faltered, I will never forget how you have helped me to see myself more clearly and I look forward to many more years of friendship and laughter.

Thank you to my Kiama Spirit Babes, Zoe and Niki, my life in Australia is much richer for your friendship having the deep and meaningful conversations, the never-ending laughter, the weekend adventures and the puppy play times that we share. Thanks for always loving me as I am.

A special thank you to Chris, Taff, Polly, Bella and Zoe for being my trusted and objective beta readers. I'm so grateful to each of you for reading my initial manuscript and providing me with valuable feedback to make this book what it is today. Your insights, care and commitment to providing constructive and objective guidance and feedback have helped me shape and communicate my message; I'm humbled that you all said yes.

Thank you to my mentor and friend, Lorna. You are a true heart-led leader, I've always admired your advocacy for female leadership and for being authentically you. No matter how challenging your workload, you have always greeted people with a smile and made time for connection; it's inspiring to watch you lead with such humility and I've no doubt your two girls have a wonderful role model in you. Thank you for saying yes to writing my Foreword, I feel truly honoured.

Thank you to Simon for always being a huge fan and for being my friend. Our relationship has evolved from being life partners to being friends and I'm so grateful that we were able to role model our conscious uncoupling and maintain a relationship of love, trust and respect for each other as we embark on new chapters of our lives.

Finally, thanks to you the reader for trusting me and sharing this journey with me. I hope you see that I'm no different from you and if there is anything that has been sparked by this book, I hope it's the belief that you have more capability than you thought and are willing to go out there and create the life you want to live. Live your truth and be unstoppable.

The Author

Glin is the founder of Heart of Human, a leadership consultancy specialising in elevating self-leadership and business performance.

As a heart-centred leader, Glin has a passion for performance while being a strong advocate for well-being. She recognises that when leaders are doing work aligned with their desires, capabilities and vision, not only are they happier and healthier, but business performance accelerates too.

Her leadership workshops and coaching of C-Level and senior executives in large corporates, including Westpac, Woolworths, Sydney University, Qantas, and George Weston Foods, are informed by over seventeen years in the corporate workplace as a qualified management accountant heading up commercial finance functions for global fast-moving consumer goods businesses, developing business strategies and driving business performance.

Leveraging her proprietary H.E.A.R.T.° Self-Leadership Method, Glin works predominantly with female business leaders who want to feel unstoppable and consciously create the leadership impact they desire and lives they love.

🌐 www.heartofhuman.com

📘 @heartofhumanofficial

in www.linkedin.com/company/heartofhuman

📷 @heartofhumanofficial

🌐 www.simplyglin.com

in www.linkedin.com/in/glinbayley

Printed in Great Britain
by Amazon

65429062R00111